"Approaching life's adversities (and opportunities) from the paradigm of the core perspective, provides me a strong directional compass, engages true values, and supports my emotional stability. Each time I engage from this perspective I experience personal growth and a strong centered self, which naturally causes the process to become intrinsic. The result I appreciate most, is my ability to respond to my world with ease and positive affect."

—Lu

"Every time, I play the game something new resonates with me and I see things more clearly. The game is fun and provides a great connection with other players. The act of delving into the realms and the close connection with core values has such an impact on my overall wellness. I highly recommend the Core Perspective-Game of Substance as a way to engage your inner core and discover your own patterns and strengths."

—Lisa

"Sandra majestically combines an earth based approach to spirituality. The tools I've used, combined with the experiences gained from the game have dramatically aided in a personal shift of direction, for which I am forever grateful."

—Steph

THE
CORE
PERSPECTIVE

A Still Point of View

SANDRA ZARUBA

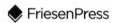 FriesenPress

Suite 300 - 990 Fort St
Victoria, BC, V8V 3K2
Canada

www.friesenpress.com

ISBN
978-1-5255-4898-7 (Hardcover)
978-1-5255-4899-4 (Paperback)
978-1-5255-4900-7 (eBook)

1. SELF-HELP, PERSONAL GROWTH, HAPPINESS

Distributed to the trade by The Ingram Book Company

Within the stillness of the core is ease.

Create more ease through a strong sense of self.

*Ease: naturalness; peacefulness; freedom or
relief from pain, anxiety, or trouble.*

Sense of Self: the knowing of who we truly are deep down inside.

The feelings of joy and happiness that make us vibrant
often elude us without a solid connection to ease. In order to
consciously connect with ease, engaging a framework for self-
discovery is most helpful. Developing a foundation of ease within
is key to the process of thinking and feeling for yourself or, in
other words, individuality.

Dedicated to

The freedom to choose our focus

In appreciation of

Life force energy
The core within
The Law of Engagement
The Law of Attraction
The unfolding
The resilient human spirit
Nature

Intention

To support the cultivation of deeper
self-awareness in everyday life

Contents

PREFACE

This book is not about comparison, but about individuality.
My hope is that by offering my personal discoveries and truths, it will spark an interest in others to expand their awareness of how to develop authenticity or individuality at ever-deepening levels in everyday life, and to support the same in children.

A core focus "sheds light" on the benefits of self-reflection, introspection, self-awareness, and energy awareness in everyday life, and allows us to see that these activities are necessary ingredients for personal growth and expansion, renewal and an enhanced level of health and well-being. A core focus also allows us to see that these "good habits" are very important to the concepts of ease, vibrancy, conscious manifestation, and the pursuit of joy and happiness.

I speak of the Law of Engagement, as I have experienced this "law" for many years, and I put a name to it that makes the most sense to me. To become conscious of this universal law, or "force to be reckoned with," requires that we be open to it, trust in it, and believe in ourselves. Be willing to self-reflect, and make shifts or changes within, and in our lives when "called" to do so.

I speak of the different energies that flow through our body and how they influence our physical, mental, and emotional well-being and our overall state of ease and vibrancy.

I remain in appreciation of all of my fellow seekers of truth, as I have drawn upon their truths in my quest to expand my own.

I remain in appreciation and very grateful to all of my friends, family, and co-workers who have allowed me to express my ongoing truths, discoveries, and ideas, over many, many years. They have been wonderful sounding boards—their opinions, suggestions, hands-on contributions, and levels of resistance have been invaluable to me and my ability to embody my truths, develop my creativity and depth perception (*to perceive from deepening levels within*).

My hope is that this book will provide a clear picture of my discoveries. I have dug deep within myself and found the importance of being conscious of the concepts of ease (*being natural and peaceful*) and vibrancy (*being full of energy and life*). I remain open to being in a world where supporting each other in being true to ourselves and others is chosen more often than not. I envision a world in which we naturally perceive from a still point of view, a place of knowing, that can bring out the best in ourselves and others with ease.

AWAKENING

To be love is to be fully engaging our own core within.

Believe in yourself – Know yourself – Be true to yourself

We are ultimately responsible for our own happiness.

To truly know yourself is to be connected with the energy of love. To be love. To be goodness. This "knowing" requires a conscious quest for deeper levels of self-awareness and higher levels of awareness of the world around us. This quest requires that we trust that, within the "mundane" of our everyday lives lies a path of self-discovery that beckons us. Embracing this path with a spirit of adventure allows for the ongoing discovery of who we truly are deep down inside. It enables us to be love (*our true authentic natures*), with all the joy and happiness that this entails.

I was awakened over twenty years ago and very quickly! By awakened, I mean that I found myself going beyond the bounds of my "normal" consciousness—outside of my "normal" existence—and into an expanded state of self-awareness and an expanded world. I see myself as an ordinary person who did not hear the beckoning from within, or who had not fully comprehended its meaning, but who had an extraordinary experience of awakening instead. This experience was an "eye opener," to say the least, and I have felt compelled to embody my truths and to offer my discoveries ever since.

At thirty-three years of age I had "attained" everything that I thought, or that I had been taught to think, would make me happy. Instead of experiencing happiness, I became increasingly frustrated with my surroundings. My overall feelings of joy were slipping away, and I was manifesting some physical symptoms of dis-ease in my body.

I continued to feel an inner urging to somehow discover what was missing in my life. Since I had always maintained a conscious connection and belief in God, or our Heavenly Father (*or Infinite Intelligence*), I strongly asked this realm the fateful questions: *What is missing in my life? Why am I so unhappy when I should be happy?* My strong heart's desires were also expressed: *Please show me what I am missing! Please help me see!* I knew that something wasn't quite right, but I just couldn't figure it out for myself.

My questions and desires had called for "change catalysts" to enter my life so that I could receive some answers. I like to refer to any person or experience that causes disruption in my world as a "catalyst." This helps me to suspend judgment of the individual or situation so that I can keep moving forward. Change most often causes anxiety and uncomfortable feelings, and it is easy to react and blame rather than to look at oneself and give thanks for the introspection and renewal opportunities.

These "change catalysts" sent me on a journey of epic proportions, a journey of self-discovery without any tools in particular, relying on my gut instincts and my "resilient spirit" to survive. My world had been turned upside down with the ultimate intention of turning me inside out! I felt like I was being cast out into the wilderness, and all I knew was that I wanted to make it "home," or at least back to something solid and known.

One thing led to another, and my life began to shift and change quickly. I unconsciously knew—or in other words, my gut instincts told me—to connect with my core, my solid ground, my internal compass for direction. As the pressure continued to build, and as I reached the end of my rope or my ability to comprehend logically what was transpiring, I gave into stillness and just prayed. I had learned the Lord's Prayer in elementary school; I had always liked it, and I could relate to it on some level, and I just began to repeat it to myself. Suddenly, I felt an internal blockage of sorts being blasted away, rather than "a veil" being lifted as described by many others. In came a flood of source energy (*the infinite*) from above that continued to flow at a pace that was impossible to ignore. This energy was filled with insights and renewal. I gained an awareness of myself and others that was far beyond anything that I could relate to in my life up to that point. I had experienced an awakening of sorts, although I did not fully grasp this notion of an "awakening" at the time. In hindsight, I see that my vibrancy level had expanded at an extraordinary pace, and I required an equal level of grounding to sustain it.

It has taken me over twenty years, and many more *less intense* catalysts, to process and comprehend this experience, to integrate this self-awareness, and to contain the flow of this expanded level of energy in a balanced way in my everyday life. I had received the answer to my questions, loud and clear. What is very apparent to me now is that what was missing in my life was a conscious, balanced, solid connection to my core within (*core energy system*) or my subtle body. Developing a balanced and strong connection to my core within has proven to be the key to my level of ease and vibrancy, and my overall feelings of comfort and joy.

The rush of energy that I experienced was filled with a conscious awareness of my multidimensional nature—that it was mine to nurture. It was terrifying and freeing at the same time. I needed to understand this new expansiveness, and I had a great desire to be able to explain this expansiveness to others. My goal remains to inspire others to connect with their inner core and the process of energy renewal, but at a much more systematic and intentional pace. The possibilities of the conscious awareness of the self or energy body on a grand scale are exciting, as more and more people attune inward.

The biggest miracle in my life to date is how this renewal allowed me to see children as they truly are, especially my two sons. Children are truly "gifts from heaven," with their own inner energetic cores intact. They are so new, fresh, loving, sweet, funny, adorable, and such individuals. They deserve to be loved unconditionally, as this is how they love us. I created the *Back to the Core Within Guidance Cards* as a supportive tool to help others open to this broader and deeper perspective when interrelating with children. This daily guidance helps us to give children the space they need to be, and to learn more about, themselves. The gifts and benefits of this approach are many, and as I incorporated this approach into my daily life, I also learned much about myself as a parent and as a person. I am still amazed at the amount of joy and personal growth that continues to open up to me from consciously engaging the wisdom of my inner core in my everyday life, especially when interrelating with children.

As my initial awakening was very sudden, the experience created an overall energy imbalance in my system (*I became even more top heavy energetically—high and light*), and with this I became very introspective as well. I had to persist in "coming down" and "surfacing" to feel and to be balanced and grounded. There was really no other choice. The flow of our life force energy slows as it moves down our body and enters the watery world of

4

our emotions and the slow moving, crystallizing, powerful energy of our physical world. Throughout my life I had lived mostly as an insightful, rather quiet person, and this imbalance created some energetic blocks at a fairly deep emotional and physical level to work through, dissipate, and ultimately overcome.

When I use the term "energetic blocks," or "blocks," I am referring to energy flows that are becoming stagnant. Rather than our energy flowing with ease through an area within, our energy develops a high level of density or opacity (*the quality or state of a body that makes it impervious to the rays of light; the relative capacity of matter to obstruct the transmission of radiant energy*). This density is a block to our free-flowing energy and nature, and usually manifests as dis-ease and suffering.

My energy blocks (*dense matter*) were created as my unconscious patterns of thought and behavior had become habitual or chronic. We all have blocks to work through (*breathing deeply without judgment while focusing on our core values*) and to dissipate (*to disperse; to disappear*) if we choose to move closer to our inner core and our authentic self. Moving through and dissipating blocks can be unsettling, but it is well worth the effort. It is truly amazing to recognize our multidimensional nature, as we become more aware of balancing our own energetic system, or our internal, higher self.

Moving closer towards inner balance has taken time and has required much persistence, courage, and faith. There have been many levels of personal resistance to this understanding, and confidence to be my authentic self in order to bring my message forward. One pattern of thought that I had to work through that had reduced my true clarity was the opinion that the material world was not friendly and safe, and that it was "flat" (*not animated—vigorous; having life*). As I moved through this thought pattern, however, I began to consciously connect with the great "Living Presence," or the source energy of our Earth Mother, the divine feminine, or the natural world, or the energy of pure love that surrounds us inside and out. I knew then that as long as I was engaging the core of my being and using my common sense, I would be safe and supported by this presence.

Given that my basic nature has always been to take everything in stride, feeling natural and at ease, I knew that I had to develop a solid basic understanding of my energy body. I needed to have a comfortable relationship with my senses, emotions, and intuition before I could feel satisfied and whole. This encouraged me to continue with my inner work and self-reflection as I went about my daily life.

Since graduating from the three-year Integrated Energy Healing Program offered by Langara College, in Vancouver, British Columbia, Canada in 2009, I have developed *The Core Perspective—A Framework for Self-Discovery*. This framework consists of two components that complement each other; *The Core Perspective—Game of Substance* and *The Core-Focused Renewal System*. I have chosen to use twenty-nine solid core values to be the focal point of both components.

The intention of both the game and the renewal system is to be hands-on, fun, and engaging. The challenge is to play the game often and to repeat the exercises of the renewal system regularly. In other words, to have core-focused renewal and living become second nature, and to have the concept of both personal and group levels of ease and vibrancy be in the forefront of everyday life. A more in-depth description of the game, the renewal system, and the twenty-nine core values is offered in the resources section of this book to learn more.

INNER CORE

The core is the central, innermost, essential, foundational part of all life.

The energy of the core is pure, infinite, bright, and vibrant.

The energy of the core is infused with a knowing of solid core values.

It is the place within.

From the perspective of the core, everything in matter is always moving towards balance in each and every moment. The most centered or balanced place within all forms of life is the inner core. From the core you can see that everything that "happens to us" happens for a reason. This reason is to keep us engaging with our core in a balanced way in order to keep us at ease, vibrant, strong, and truly alive. Our growth and evolution, both as individuals and collectively, depends upon this balance. To engage and feel our energetic inner core in everything that we think, say, and do is the true meaning of being fully alive—being totally engaged with ourselves and with the flow of life force energy.

The more we engage our inner core or "knowing" in a balanced way, the more expansive and abundant our lives become for us and those around us. This innate knowing helps us to recognize and clear/remove chronic thought and behavioral patterns that no longer serve us. The opposite of recognizing our patterns is said to be true if we go through life connecting to "shoulds" and "should nots"—ingrained, unconscious patterns of thought and behavior that narrow and reduce our lives. Our inner core can become overshadowed by these unconscious chronic patterns that create energy blocks. Many examples found in nature give us clues about our own true nature and the value of our core within.

"Never does nature say one thing and wisdom another."

Juvenal, Roman poet late 1st and early 2nd century AD

More often than not, we give very little thought to our energetic core. Allowing our core to become "nonexistent" through lack of awareness and attention creates an unconscious void in our life. This void in itself creates contraction and an overall lack of health and well-being on many levels. Rather than our world becoming more energized and full of life, we find our world becoming more and more lifeless. Unconscious thought and behavioral patterns that become chronic also create the dynamic of being "set in our ways." Without a solid connection to our inner core where our life force energy is flowing, it becomes less possible to create chemistry, generate attraction, or manifest our heart's desires. It is also interesting to take note that there have been a number of great societies that have disappeared, along with what appears to be the disappearance of their solid core values —their moral core.

When we make the conscious choice to engage the core of our being more fully, we begin to feel a lot more than what we are used to feeling—we are engaging our body's wisdom to a much fuller extent. We are sensing the core of our being more often and in all circumstances. We come to the realization that we have an inner voice that is helping to guide us, as an individual, every step of the way. This inner voice is our higher self and this flow of energy is infused with a knowing of solid core values.

> *"Listen to the voice which is without sound."*
>
> Author unknown

If we do heed the wisdom of our inner voice, we may encounter energy blocks within that may feel uncomfortable. This identifies patterns of thought or behavior that no longer serve us. The key is to breathe through and dissipate the blocks that have materialized by "hanging on to" our outdated ways. We may also feel the gravity of knowing that we must look to ourselves for answers and to take responsibility for our actions and our own happiness.

We know if we are perceiving from the core of our being, if we feel a sense of shifting, lightness, renewal, hope, and joy. An overall feeling that all is well in the present moment indicates that we are engaging the core of our being and following the guidance of our inner voice. If we resist our inner voice and give in to the "shoulds" and "should nots"—and negativity, blame, impatience, and temptation—our body will let us know through feelings of physical discomfort, and mental and emotional distress. We will also know by what we are attracting into our lives.

Engaging the core of our being is a rediscovery for many of us, and during this ongoing process we will experience both satisfaction and frustration. As we work through (*breathing deeply without judgment while focusing on core values*), dissipate (*to disperse; to disappear*) our blockages (*dense matter*) and to transcend (*go beyond; rise above*) our outdated thought and behavioral patterns, our inner core grows in strength. We will feel more ease, inner verve, joy, and sense of direction on a regular basis. As we become more self-aware, we will develop a greater understanding of where we are in our process, in the present moment. This understanding helps us to remain focused and optimistic.

We know whether our thoughts and behavioral patterns are no longer serving us well by how we feel, physically and emotionally. If we are feeling heavy, dull, depressed, tense, impatient, debilitated, controlling, or if we have manifestations of dis-ease in our body, then we know that there are patterns that no longer serve in supporting ease and vibrancy. We will need to discover and dissipate the blocks created by these patterns, and be open to something new. Life brings us experiences that will pressure us to change our patterns, dissipate our blocks, and to let go and grow. Sometimes these experiences can feel like a storm is blowing through, but it is good to keep in mind "that this too shall pass," and "it is an ill wind that blows no good." Trusting in the process and allowing something new to develop is very important. There may be short-term pain, but there will always be long-term gain. Changing our patterns and dissipating blocks creates change in our lives. Many of us resist and fear change, and we may prefer our patterns, even though they are creating dis-ease and are depleting possibility and growth in our life.

> *"The only thing we have to fear…is fear itself."*
>
> Franklin D. Roosevelt, 32nd President of the United States,
> First Inaugural Address, USA, 1933

Society puts pressure on the individual, over time, to conform to societal norms and conventions. Conforming has certain advantages in the short run, but in the long run, unconscious conformity removes a conscious sense of self. When self-confidence is eroded and the natural ability to listen to our inner voice is clouded, our higher self or core guidance is reduced along with the ability to make wise choices. Unconscious conformity is very depleting in many ways for individuals, and for society as a whole. The challenge for many is to live through the uncomfortable feelings of fear and uncertainty that may arise as one is faced with changing the patterns of unconscious conformity.

When we do not know who we are to any great extent, it is very challenging for us to know what we want out of our lives. Our sense of direction is eroded, and we are easily convinced, manipulated, or controlled. Often one hears of the phrase "ignorance is bliss," but this ignorance is not knowing who we truly are deep down inside. Unconscious living, just "going through the motions" of daily life, without self-reflection, comes at a big price. When we live this kind of life, we are engaging a fraction of our potential, and are self-imposing limits to our greater happiness and fulfillment. It has been mentioned by many fellow seekers that we have only scratched the surface of what humanity is capable of becoming, and that the universe is designed to support our desires that come from within us.

Sickness and dis-ease are not our natural states of being. Health and ease are our natural states. From the core perspective, it is useful to contemplate the meaning of the words "chronic" and "ease," the prefix "dis," and the definition of a chronic condition.

(Definitions have been compiled from a variety of dictionaries.)

chronic: constant; habitual; inveterate (*having a particular habit, activity, or interest that is long-established and unlikely to change*).

ease: the condition of being comfortable or relieved; absence of difficulty or hardship; freedom from pain, worry, or agitation; naturalness; state of rest and relaxation; to lessen the strain, pressure, or tension of all situations; to reduce the difficulty or trouble of; to move or navigate slowly and carefully; to appear effortless.

dis: a Latin prefix meaning "apart," "asunder," "away," "utterly," or having a privative (*marked by the absence, removal, or loss of some quality normally present*), negative, or reversing force.

The perspective of the core asks that, on a regular basis, we focus on dissipating energetic blocks created by thought and behavioral patterns that are no longer serving us. This process of dissipating helps us to gradually remove dense matter/energy blocks created by chronic patterns of thought and behavior. These blocks are reflected in our physical body, the flow of our lives, and they ultimately affect our feelings of joy and happiness. Chronic patterns are the hardest to see and the most challenging to overcome. By engaging with our core, or the center of our being, on a regular basis, anything is possible. Connecting and engaging our core energy flow animates and exercises all of our organs, including our brain. The first step lies in the matter of choice. Choose to connect, engage, and grow, or choose to retain patterns that no longer serve and contract.

When the clouds are finally dissipated and the sun shines through, we all feel uplifted and renewed. *Can you imagine a world where the weather patterns are static and the sun remains overshadowed by the clouds?* As we shift our patterns of thought and behavior that no longer serve us (*those we have outgrown*), we begin the process of dissipating the blocks created by these patterns and allowing the energy of our core to flow more fully, rejuvenating our cells and organs. All of our senses become infused with more vibrancy and optimism as well. We can learn so much from nature. To create a life of ease and vibrancy requires that we focus on becoming increasingly self-aware and engaged as we journey through life.

**See your reflection in the elements of Mother Earth
and join the energy movement.**

ENERGY BODY

The flow of life force energy and solid core values go hand in hand.
This "match made in heaven" creates a "knowing"
system of self-discovery.

Core-focused renewal and living asks that we develop a basic understanding of our core energy structure, how it feels to us, what it means to us, and what core values amplify aspects of our energy body when we connect with them. In developing and understanding our core, we create depth as we connect with our core. This basic awareness of our energy body, or subtle body, helps us to move through and process challenges in everyday life, smoothly and with our integrity intact.

The depth of knowledge and understanding of our physical body and energy body is limitless, but even a basic awareness of both can enhance our lives greatly and is key to the process of conscious energy renewal. Most of us have a basic knowledge of our physical body. I have found the book, *The Polarity Process Energy as A Healing Art* by Franklyn Sills, most helpful for developing a basic knowledge of our core energy system (*the mainstream of our life force energy, our driving force and solid foundation*). The *Polarity Process Energy as A Healing Art* draws most specifically on the work of Dr. Stone, a great pioneer and healer. The following descriptions of our energy body (*prior to the diagram of our energy body*) are primarily paraphrased from *The Polarity Process Energy as A Healing Art*.

Our core energy system includes six energy centers or chakras, five elements, five oval fields, and three linking currents: Ida, Pingala, and Shushumna. The six energy centers are traditionally called chakras, and they can be visualized as pulsating orbs that both suck energy in and push energy out of their centers. They are the source of energy flow for all the Five Element energy pulses. The six chakras or energy centers (*from top to bottom*) are named for the quality of energy that emanates from them: Brow, Ether, Air, Fire, Water, and Earth (*they are also commonly known as: Third Eye, Throat, Heart, Solar Plexus, Sacral, and Root*). As energy steps down from center to center, there is a narrowing of the field of consciousness and a lowering of energy intensity at each successive phase. Each center acts like a two-way electrical transformer that steps down electrical voltage from a higher intensity to a lower intensity and back up again.

Two waves of positive and negative energies expand outwards from the Brow Center to form two pulsating currents. These are traditionally called the Pingala (*right channel; positive quality*) and the Ida (*left channel; negative quality*) currents. These expand outward, reach their point of completion, and then undergo a contractive phase. They are pulled together to form a new neutral center in the throat, the Ether Center. Between the two centers, a third channel also arises. This is a neutral channel, which is physically located in the spine. It is traditionally called the Sushumna (*central channel; neutral quality*).

These three currents, the Pingala, Ida, and Sushumna, represent the three phases of movement of the Gunas (*three major types of flow*) in their positive, negative, and neutral qualities. They spiral down to form each energy center or chakra where they intersect. In other words where the currents are drawn together, a chakra or energy center forms.

From the Ether Center downwards, the three phases of movement of the Gunas continue, and four additional centers are formed, which are named Air, Fire, Water and Earth. They are thus named as at each center a different quality of energy arises. The quality of energy at each center is called an element and relates to the function and processes of life which that center governs. The five elements or energy relationships come into play and these five qualities of energy interweave to form our subtle energy patterns.

At each energy center or chakra, fields of energy arise, which Dr. Stone called the "oval fields." These oval fields arise from and surround the chakras. For energy to move, there must be a field to support its movement. These pulsating "motor" fields provide a ground or medium that allow the movement of other energy patterns across them. The oval fields are named for the dominant quality of movement through them.

Looking at the oval fields from top to bottom:

- The Fire oval of the head relates to the fire of energy coming into form. It is the fire of intelligence and the clarity of insight.

- The Ether oval of the throat is about space and communication.

- The Air oval of the chest is about breath and heartfelt feelings.

- The Earth oval of the solar plexus is about strength and power. It is about how we use our force, whether it be for digestion or for action.

- The Water oval of the lower abdomen is about the grounding flow of energy, and our connection to the world.

Each field/center/chakra represents a unique energy and consciousness, and with each step down, there is more restriction in the quality of consciousness and limitation in vibration. All five qualities and flows of energy are found everywhere in the body, but each is predominant in its own sphere. The relationship between the elements and their energy patterns are dynamic ones. At every place a field meets or changes into another field, there is a transition, and a major change in energy. Looking at these oval fields, their transitions and relationships, we can begin to see how these fields become physical and underlie (*form the basis of*) our form. The key to this understanding lies in the body's connective tissue and fascia, as it is all continuous. A restriction or imbalance in one area gets transferred to other areas via this continuity.

Crown Chakra/Vortex
Third Eye Chakra/Brow Center/Fire Oval
Throat Chakra/Ether Center/Ether Element/Ether Oval
Heart Chakra/Air Center/Air Element/Air Oval
Solar Plexus Chakra/Fire Center/Fire Element/Earth Oval
Sacral Chakra/Water Center/Water Element/Water Oval
Root Chakra/Earth Center/Earth Element/Water Oval
Base Vortex

These oval fields/centers/chakras are always communicating with each other, and they send out signals prompting us to engage with our inner core in a balanced way. As we grow and mature and continue to perceive from the core of our being as we grow through life, we are developing a conscious connection to source energy (*the infinite*) that is the core of our physical self and beyond. There are chakras/vortexes that reside just above and below these six major energy spheres. The vortex that resides at the crown of the head and opens upward is commonly referred to as the Crown Chakra, and the vortex that I have sensed residing at the base of the tail bone/coccyx and opening downward is known to me as the Base Vortex.

I often refer to these two energetic connections as the connections to our "Source Parents"—our Heavenly Father or God, and our Mother Earth or Gaia. The connection to the source opens the pathway to insights and higher consciousness and the ability to consciously "core-create" (*embodiment of our core as we create*) with the "Great Living Presence." The energy that is present in and around all life forms here on Earth, is always moving toward more life, fuller functioning, and more abundance for all.

Looking at these energies superficially, they are all one, and we often speak of energy only in terms of levels, and sometimes by color, in daily conversation. Taking a slightly closer look at our energy body, however, allows us to discover how we can consciously support the maintenance of a balanced and renewing flow of life force energy within our system, and that will be reflected in our surroundings.

Accept the paradigm of a spherical energy body and become part of the age of self-discovery.

Physical accidents, incidents, or repetitive activities can have a major affect on the free-flowing nature of our subtle energy body. Anything that shocks or impedes the body shocks or impedes the entire system, and vice versa. Patterns of thought and behavior that no longer serve us also create energy blocks (*dense matter*) that reduce the free-flowing nature of energy—and life itself. In general, energy needs to be flowing freely within for life to be flowing freely without.

Chronic, unconscious patterns of thought and behavior are usually considered to be the most "dense." They can create the biggest energy blocks, and they have the potential to do the most damage to our physical, emotional, and mental states. For example, if we do not grow past the need to fulfill our own personal wants, and we find ourselves in close relationships, we will experience many power struggles with others. Power struggles are always lose-lose. They are very hard on our nerves, our emotions, and ultimately, our energetic and physical bodies. Thinking about our own needs without regard for the needs of others helps create these power struggles and often manifest as high blood pressure, sleep deprivation, low sex drive, overeating, digestive disorders, depression, and anxiety for everyone involved.

If we notice these symptoms, it is wise to look at our patterns of thought and behavior. We will most certainly find one, two, or three behaviors or patterns that are no longer serving us. Our true essence is a "knowing" of solid core values. This is who we truly are at our core. We have an innate (*inborn, natural*) and deep-seated need to stay connected to this place of knowing at all times. This place within is the <u>mainstream of our life force energy</u> and our driving force, and it determines our levels of ease, vibrancy, growth, and expansion.

The stimulus for growth and expansion lies within. As we look within, we see without.

As we develop increased energy awareness, we are able to detect the subtle signals and signs being transmitted to us with much greater ease. Our ability to see, feel, and experience our surroundings (*our extrasensory perception*), increases markedly, and our ability to hear and act upon our inner voice becomes much more immediate and natural. We learn to pause and attune inward when we come across situations that make us feel uncertain or uncomfortable. We will know that, if we feel uncomfortable with what we are thinking, doing, or saying, it is because we are going against our own personal knowing, and that if we continue, we will create dis-ease within our system.

Energy awareness gives pressure situations an entirely new meaning. Pressure is actually a gift of opportunity. When we encounter pressure situations, this is when we can do our inner work, introspection, and self-discovery. The core value exercise of *The Core-Focused Renewal System* is a simplified practical tool for learning how to respond to situations by engaging our core values and our inner core more fully.

Exercise example: Focus on a current pressure situation, determine the ten core values that are pertinent, reflect again on the pressure, re-evaluate the values and choose four, reflect again, and choose the one needed to connect with. Embody the essence of this crucial core value to attain the feeling that you are looking for within.

The core-creating exercise of *The Core-Focused Renewal System* is also a simplified and practical tool for understanding more clearly what our heart truly desires.

Exercise example: Focus on two desires, determine the one of most importance. As you embody this desire notice the feelings that you are generating. If this desire is aligned with your core within, you will be experiencing feelings such as joy and elation. If you are feeling anything other than joy and elation, know that you still have resistance attached to your desire. Accept the resistance and use your breath to quiet your mind, allowing room for the new to enter and to take shape.

Both aspects of responding and understanding are very freeing energetically, physically, mentally, and emotionally. Understanding our energy body through words alone is impossible. *The Core Perspective-Game of Substance* is a fun and challenging way to engage and to learn about the process of developing deeper self-awareness and energy renewal in everyday life—all while spending a couple of uplifting hours with others, playing together. As the game is played, one may feel the weight and frustration of holding onto patterns of thought and behavior that no longer serve. It is wonderful to experience the feelings of relief and accomplishment as the patterns are lifted—as the blocks are cleared—through a focus on solid core values. When the game is played more often, a true sense of the process of energy renewal in everyday life is developed. This awareness sinks in a little deeper and expands a little more each and every time the game is played. The process becomes innate.

Further description and information about the resources mentioned in this chapter are found on pages 87–96.

An in-depth list and definitions of the twenty-nine core values used in the resources are found on pages 97–99.

LAW OF ENGAGEMENT

The spiral is a sacred symbol that reflects the pattern of growth and evolution that emanates from the core.

The core is love.

Be love.

From the perspective of the core, our system is always moving towards balance. It is governed by homeostasis (*a natural regulator that seeks a stable, constant condition, equilibrium and balance on a moment-to-moment basis*). I believe that through intuition, observation, and common sense, the entire universe is always moving towards this same balance. The term Law of Engagement describes a force that responds on our behalf to allow us to continue to connect to and engage with our inner core in a balanced way. The spiral is a sacred symbol that reflects the pattern of growth and evolution that emanates from the core. The symbol of a spiral is found everywhere in nature and in ancient cultures throughout the world.

From the perspective of the core, you can see that everything happens for a reason, and that all is well. The Law of Engagement supports us in becoming who we truly are, or all that we can be. Our true self is balanced, centered, and aligned with our core within. Our inner core is pure, infinite, bright, and vibrant and is infused with a knowing of solid core values. Our personal energetic balance and level of connection is a reflection of our own personal freedom to choose. Freedom to choose creates balance. A lack of the freedom to choose creates imbalance.

The Law of Engagement tirelessly helps us to stay connected or to become more connected to our core in a balanced way in our everyday lives. I give thanks to this law every day—without it, I would be lost and I would not have been able to "pull myself together" in certain circumstances. I refer to the conscious process of engagement as "core-focused renewal and living," which asks us to attune inward in all of our pressure situations in order to see and feel the parts of ourselves that need our loving attention. The relative ease of this process is a reflection of our co-operation with, or our resistance to, the Law of Engagement. It is also a reflection of our current level of connection to our own personal knowing or self-awareness. If you have not been conscious of core-focused renewal, don't be hard on yourself or remain in resistance to this process; just make a promise that you will become more self-aware going forward, so that your life and the lives of those around you may be filled with more ease and vibrancy.

The basics of being balanced at an energetic level requires that the six major energy centers of our core engage with each other at a relatively similar level. This balance is what makes up what we often refer to as our soul, or our self. A balanced state allows for the healthy flow of life force energy (*prana, mana, or chi*) both within our body and our immediate surroundings (*within and without*).

The smooth inner flow allows us to retain a healthy connection to source energy (*the infinite*) that is beyond our physical body, and allows our energy body (*subtle body*) to renew itself on an ongoing basis. This allows our physical body to invigorate itself at the same time. The greater the prana levels in our bodies, the more elasticity and pliability is present both physically and mentally. We become increasingly animated. The alternative is that we become denser and more resistant to change, and the flow of our own life force energy diminishes.

A connection to source energy (*the infinite*) above refers to the insights that filter down to us through our Crown Chakra. Have you ever found yourself asking, *"Where did that thought come from? How come I didn't think of that before?"* Have you found yourself thinking that you just had an *"Aha!"* moment, and now everything made sense? Has anyone asked you, *"How do you know that?"* And you hear yourself saying, *"I don't know; I just know."*

Maintain inner balance and keep an open mind.

A connection to source energy below refers to how we are engaging the life force energy here on Earth, through our connection to our Base Vortex and our surroundings. *Where are our actions coming from? Are they connected to the core and core values, self-love, or inner voice?* If they are, then they will be connected to, and supported by, the universal love energy that surrounds us and is coming from all life forms here on Earth. The Law of Attraction says that if we ask from the place of knowing, then what we ask for will be given, drawn to us or manifested in our surroundings.

Maintain inner balance and act with integrity.

As we engage our integrity and insightful mind, we naturally become an observer and a core-creator (*embodiment of our core as we create*) which is often labeled as "being real" or "living our truths." We find that our desires will always be aligned with serving the greater good, as well as ourselves. This is what true maturity or blossoming is all about, and what true freedom really means—the freedom to be our authentic self. Our desires will begin to manifest or "come about" with relative ease. They will be aligned with our inner core and supported by the divine energies—the great "Living Presence of the Universe."

> **When our thinking and feeling energies are in unison we attune to a knowing. Do from this place of knowing. A place of balance within.**

If we are coming from, or going through, our life from the perspective of our personality and ego, to a great extent we remain in resistance to change. Then the Law of Engagement may become known to us as the "School of Hard Knocks," or worse. If we come from the perspective of our personality and ego, but remain open to change, then the Law of Engagement may become known to us as "getting knocked around" or "rolling with the punches"— getting to what is real or to engage our authentic self.

We are created to grow beyond the self-absorbed wants of our ego. If we find ourselves being knocked around, or we feel like we are getting hammered on, this is likely the urging and nudging from within to change patterns of thought and behavior that are no longer serving us, and that are being ignored, buried, repressed, or denied. This is a sign that we are continuing to veer off course, to move further and further from our center, our core within, our core values, who we truly are. The energy of the Law of Engagement will continue to work tirelessly on our behalf and will manifest in our lives as very challenging and trying situations, or will bring forth very challenging catalysts to bring us closer towards balance.

During the process of living an engaged life, we must remember not to worry or focus on outcomes, but rather, to focus on the feeling we are seeking, and allow things to unfold. The key is that, through the positive feelings within ourselves, we begin to feel better, feel good, satisfied, peaceful, or whatever feeling we are seeking in the present moment. We take responsibility for our own happiness and our own personal choices.

As core-focused living becomes second-nature to us, we become consciously aware of the presence of the Law of Engagement, our level of ease, and our vibrancy on a daily basis, and we are able to tap into and "see" the world of renewable source energy.

This world is truly full of life and relative ease, and can be described in many colorful ways: expansive, multidimensional, stimulating, creative, abundant, exciting, full of promise, trust, hope, movement, freedom to choose, discovery of self and others, joy, health and well-being, self-expression, challenges, connections, motivation, purpose, peace, beauty, strength, openings, renewal, and accepting.

One of the most miraculous things about the world of renewable source energy is that it is within our grasp. Every choice we make can be core-focused or not, true or not. Choose wisely! As more of us choose wisely more often, this world of ease and vibrancy will expand exponentially. In other words, "go forth and multiply."

When we ask the universe for something, it is a reflection that we have desires, visions, goals, dreams, and that we remain engaged in life. When we ask, "it" is given, as long as we remain open to receive it. When we are in the receptive mode, we will be given insights and learning experiences to help us connect with our desires. We may not get exactly what we "thought" we were asking for, but we will get exactly what we need for our "highest good." I am often surprised at what it is that I actually need, but it is always pure perfection and is often better for me than what I

actually asked for in the first place. Life often does not give us what
we think we want, but if we are persistent in our pursuits, we will
get exactly what we need. Trusting in the unfolding is one of the
keys to the process of conscious manifestation.

We also need to be careful what we ask for, and consider if the
request is coming from our authentic self. Maintaining our sense
of humor as we move through any challenges that may arise is
most beneficial.

Core-focused living is a challenging and expanded way of living.
For many, breathing deeply through uncomfortable feelings
(*without judgment*) when they arise is often required and very
helpful. It is not always easy to move through and dissipate energy
blocks created by patterns of thought and behavior that no longer
serve us. Some blockages can be very deeply rooted. This dense
matter will be dissipated as we shift our patterns, and it is well
worth the effort every time. If we are true to ourselves, or our core
within, we will always receive what we value.

> *"Your worth consists of what you are*
> *and not what you have."*
>
> Thomas Edison (1847-1931), an American inventor and business man

The dynamic of synchronicity *(the simultaneous occurrence
of events that appear significantly related but have no discernible
causal connection)* appears to surface in the world of deepening
self-awareness. Synchronicity appears to accompany the commit-
ted person who is following through with desires that are coming
from the "still place"—our core within. Synchronicity, or the
appearance of a coincidence, most often seems to occur when we
are encountering much resistance to having our desires manifest
or "come to pass." Our resolve to keep moving towards our desires
and dreams is beginning to weaken. When we experience a synchronistic event it often feels profound, joyous, or incredibly lucky

and gives us a needed boost of energy, optimism, hope, and the belief that anything is possible.

I believe that the mere act of being open to synchronicities is a way to help us move forward and avoid remaining with old patterns of thought and behavior that no longer serve us. It also helps us to remember that we are not alone in our pursuits. Our offerings may turn out to be another person's synchronistic event—one that will help them to move forward in their life. In other words, keep going and never quit when pursuing a heart's desire. Keeping this in mind helps remove patterns of feeling rejected or taking things personally. These two patterns—fear of rejection and fear of being judged—stop many people from continuing to pursue their goals, desires, and dreams.

Appreciate all that is in the present moment. The true power of appreciation resides in first asking for something from a place of self-love and acceptance. Asking needs to come from our inner voice, or higher self—the "still place." Once we've asked (*for something*), we need to remain thankful for everything that comes into our lives. Practice the knowing that there will be good in all things and that they will be expansive. Actively express this to ourselves and to others. Keep focusing on our wish or desire, and remain open to receiving it. The Source, the Great Living Presence, the Great Mystery, or the Infinite Intelligence, will bring us what we need to make us happy. Happiness is most abundantly found in our balanced and deepening state of being. Sometimes we receive exactly what we asked for, and at other times, what we receive is even better.

It is wise to remember that remaining in appreciation and acceptance helps to keep our vibrancy levels high, opens doors, and keeps us open to receive all that is good. The ease of living from the core perspective is typically in direct relation to the age at which one begins. In other words, the sooner the better, but it is never too late. It is never too late to give the best that we have in the present moment. The mere act of trying our best has an energy with a high vibration that will help "clear the air" and improve the atmosphere of any encounter, occasion, or event.

We all have this in common: an inner urge to do and to feel our best in the present moment. When we do and feel our best, we emanate happiness and look our best. Seeing things from the perspective of the core creates a life and a world of "relative ease." Developing a lifestyle of core-focused renewal and living, early in life, allows this style of living to become second nature as we grow through life. If we make the choice to attune inward more often, we will need to be gentle and patient with ourselves and with others to maintain and grow our ease and vibrancy levels.

It is wise to always keep our strengths and positive qualities in mind. They are there for us to use and to enjoy. These are our gifts, and they help us to succeed in everything that we pursue. Our gifts can be seen as a beautiful and colorful "icing on the cake," rather than who we truly are. Our higher self or inner voice persistently sends us messages and feelings that are designed to protect our integrity, our wholeness, and individuality. The creative mind focuses on the bigger picture, thus helping us to rise above our fears and perceived limitations. To trust our own sense of what is right for us is key for renewal and stability. Who we are and what we do will begin to fulfill an even higher purpose than our personal enjoyment. Because of our thoughts and actions, the world is filled with more ease and vibrancy.

I believe that the human spirit is a reflection of our will to remain vibrant while here on Earth. Our soul is the core of our being, our subtle energy body, and the source of our higher self, or inner voice, and the deeper part of who we truly are.

Our soul is felt throughout our body, recognized by our insightful mind. It is expressed through our desire to be love and be loved. Our personality reflects our gifts at a more superficial, or shallow, level. Our spirit and soul are expressed through our individual personalities.

> *"The human spirit goes forth from the beginning to embody every faculty, every thought, every emotion, which belongs to it in appropriate events."*

Ralph Waldo Emerson (1803-1882), Essay 1-History, self published, para. 2, USA, 1841

If we have a strong soul connection but an underdeveloped personality, the qualities of our soul may often stay secluded within us. Alternatively, if we have a strong personality, but an underdeveloped soul connection we may create a lot of false hopes and illusions. The resilient human spirit is always seeking ways that allow for the essence of the core to emerge through the personality. A great spirit reflects the whole—all aspects; mind, body, and soul—coming into play in a balanced way. Balance is the key.

PROCESS OF ENGAGEMENT

To be in love is to be fully engaging our own core within
and to be engaging with the core of another.

Growth and expansion emanate from the core. The essence of
something—the inward nature of anything—underlies its
manifestations. To be in love with another being is to fully engage
our own core, and through mutual attraction, engage with the
core of another. This may also be referred to as being with our
soulmate, or experiencing a soul connection. To be love and to be
loved. To see and to be seen.

As core-focused renewal and living becomes second nature,
partnering with a soulmate or being truly engaged will become
much more commonplace. Life that reflects all that this entails
would be beautiful to observe and to experience. We would naturally be drawn to a soulmate and a soulmate to us.

Can you imagine being in a world where everyone is feeling satisfied with their partners? Where the family unit remains intact and healthy? Where pressure situations are seen as growth opportunities, and everyone chooses to participate?

Can you imagine the relative ease of this situation and life? Can you imagine the reduction of dis-ease and suffering, and the increase in vibrancy and joy for everyone?

How do we develop a soul connection? The process of engagement can be viewed as a step-by-step process for developing true clarity (*seeing things as they truly are, not our opinionated view of how they are*) and a practical understanding (*representing a deeper level than simple knowledge*).

Step 1: Know ourselves. Ideally, self-discovery begins in childhood, and it is very natural to look inward and self-reflect.

Step 2: Know that attraction is just the initial "hook." The stronger the attraction, the bigger the hook. Adding drugs and alcohol into the mix creates false illusions and adds challenges. Take ourselves seriously. Remain authentic.

Step 3: Know that we can only affect a change from within. Remind ourselves that power struggles are a lose-lose proposition that guarantee loss. Thinking that we can change someone else to suit us better is a pattern of thought that will not serve well.

Step 4: Know that if we overlook the process of engagement, we will open a door to the world of depletion, rather than expansion and renewal.

Step 5: Move slowly and thoughtfully through the process of engagement. Consciously connect with the major energy spheres within and heed any warning signals in the form of uncomfortable thoughts and feelings that may arise.

Step 6: Create more space if resistance or uncomfortable feelings are encountered. Space can be created physically, or by true self-expression. Take a step back, <u>do not</u> participate in resistance through suppression of challenging feelings or through power struggles. Be willing to be vulnerable.

Step 7: Accept any differences. Accept that they are real. Accept that change happens slowly. Accept that we can only shift and change ourselves. Accept that both persons must retain their own integrity.

Step 8: Be patient with ourselves and with others. Wait until both persons agree on what the differences are. Wait until both are willing to do some personal introspection and shifting to bridge the gap.

Step 9: Be cautious. Enjoy the similarities and the good stuff, but keep an eye on the gap. Be conscious of whether the gap is widening or narrowing. Our inner voice will let us know by how we are feeling. We cannot allow ourselves to be disrespected, undermined, discounted, coerced, manipulated, used, or bullied.

Step 10: Maintain authenticity. If we need to create more space, do so. Remember that the more challenging the process of engagement, the more growth opportunities are being presented. It is also a reflection of our lack of self-awareness to begin with, or in many cases, how much alcohol or drugs were consumed, creating illusions, when we engaged our partner. As we all become increasingly core-focused and authentic, becoming engaged will be much simpler and more full of ease.

Step 11: Seek true clarity. If needed, step back, express our truth—we will receive more clarity. Both persons need to see, know, and feel the gap to even agree to work on it. Often, once the gap is seen and felt more clearly, we realize that we are from different worlds. Many factors, including our upbringing, may identify that the gap is truly insurmountable in this lifetime. In other words, there are irreconcilable differences. Respect these differences and the power they have to create anxiety and turmoil within ourselves and our lives.

Step 12: Love ourselves enough to step away and disengage if necessary. If the gap between the two persons is truly insurmountable, this will be seen, felt, and known through our inner being. Give thanks to life for the growth opportunity and thank our partner involved in the process of engagement, and "let bygones be bygones."

It is often challenging to let go, but it is necessary to let go in order to grow and move on. It can be especially hard to disengage when the personality and physical attraction levels are very high. To create more ease in these situations, amplify the core values of acceptance and appreciation. If this is done, everyone will maintain their integrity, at whatever level they are at in the present moment, and each will have a much better idea of who they truly are, going forward. True clarity allows the hook to be released with relative ease, and we are set free. Everyone will have moved on, and we will soon be open to other experiences. The chances of both people attracting partners that they are more compatible with next time around will be markedly increased.

If, on the other hand, the gap is closing, we will have gained in countless ways, and we will have grown as individuals, and together as partners. If both persons are self-aware, the choice of a partner will be wise, the process of engagement will contain relative ease, and the chemistry will be life-enhancing and sustainable. If we are fortunate enough to be thus engaged, we can enjoy the great and countless moments of joy and happiness.

Sustaining the chemistry of a relationship adds to the je ne sais quoi ("*I don't know what*") as time goes on. The initial attraction involves chemistry and is often based on personality traits and physical traits. If the process of engagement ensues, both partners consciously bring their souls (*the inner core of their beings*) into the mix. They bring a deeper level of self-awareness and energy, and work to build a solid container and foundation for the chemistry to flourish. They are developing a soulmate connection. Both people in the relationship are being authentic.

To bring soul or self into the mix, we need to know ourselves at some level, hopefully at an equal level to our partner. We need to continue to listen to our inner voice for guidance, and attune into and engage our main energy spheres using our core values. This results in a solid harmonious connection that both partners feel. If there is a disconnection or imbalance among any of our energy spheres and core values, we will feel some resistance within.

When this resistance happens, it is tempting to initiate a power struggle with our partner, but power struggles are always lose-lose. We need to express our truths, thus creating space and admitting to the gap. Then both people need to make decisions—jointly— to work at bridging the gap or work at disengaging. A slow and steady pace is filled with the most ease. We need to take ourselves seriously; engaging with another is definitely not a game. It may lead to short-term pain, but always long-term gain.

The process of engagement truly involves appreciation and acceptance, along with being insightful. It can be very hard, and we experience disappointment when things do not work out as expected. While we retain our integrity and remain true to ourselves, distance may be seen and felt as true unfolding takes place. Accept and appreciate all of these feelings and the experience in order to progress. Non-acceptance or resistance creates the "kicking and screaming" syndrome. Eventually both individuals will see that it is best to create some distance (*space*).

When we are attracted to someone and work through the process of engagement, and there are no large gaps remaining that create dis-ease within ourselves, we will have created a strong container for our joined chemistry to grow and stay balanced. The container or relationship includes the attraction of personality, physical traits, and the core or soul of both individuals. We will have found a soulmate; we will be truly engaged, and we can look forward to increased joie de vivre (*joy of living*), which will be generated naturally and with ease.

A long-term relationship goal is to "core-create" (*embodiment of our core as we create*) with another person with relative ease. The most rewarding relationships are generally soulmate relationships in which both individuals are fully engaged at their own personal levels, and both are consciously aware of taking responsibility for their own integrity and respecting the integrity of the other. The most challenging relationships happen when one person is not fully engaged and is unconscious of this fact. The drag on the other person to compensate for the less-than-complete engagement of their partner is quite real. The whole is greater than the sum of its parts, but the whole must represent two balanced parts to be authentic and sustainable with relative ease.

If we disregard the process of engagement, the unconsciousness of a partner may be overlooked in order to enjoy the attraction traits. Then power struggles, a natural next tendency, ensue—an uneasy mechanism that attempts to create harmony or balance. This attempt at balance, however, is merely an illusion, is always lose-lose, and is repressive. Power struggles are an effort to either wake up or repress an aspect that is creating strain or unease. What "renewal" asks us to do is to stay with integrity and recognize the level of balance or imbalance. This allows us to reflect, grow, and if in agreement, to engage one another in bridging the gap.

The process of engagement helps both individuals to see themselves at deepening levels. Then it all boils down to conscious choice. Or seen another way, it creates a natural separation, or increased space for both. The Law of Engagement will keep encouraging us to gain balance within, so that we may grow and move on naturally, or even better, to become more consciously self-aware and grow together.

At this time in our evolution, there are many separations as we all search for equality, and this needs to be seen as positive growth, no matter how challenging. If we choose to turn a blind eye to what we are observing about ourselves, we will still have grown through conscious awareness. If after we become conscious of any imbalance and try to partner again without making any changes within, we will get a deeper understanding of the futility of doing so. It seems to be a pattern for many of us to keep trying the "same old way" again and again, while hoping for different outcomes.

After we become aware of our own imbalance and accept it, then we can make a conscious choice. We can choose to stay on the road of narrowing and depleting for a while longer (*or indefinitely*), or we can choose growth and expansion and new opportunities through conscious core-focused renewal and living. A core focus will summon a deepening of inner balance and true clarity (*depth perception or extrasensory perception*).

Partnering with another person is a great opportunity for enjoyment, but it is also a great responsibility. The challenges of the process of engagement are in direct relation to our natural level of ease within ourselves. This does not mean that we are ever "finished products," but that we are self-aware enough to self-manage, and to take responsibility for ourselves and our own happiness.

Our energetic balance or imbalance creates a certain level of ease and vibrancy. If we have developed sufficient self-awareness to be aligned with our inner core, we are emanating a state of balance and will attract other people who are emanating this balance. The process of engagement will ensue with much more ease. As we get to know one another, we discover our compatibility at a deeper level of the soul or self. During close, personal interaction, conflict, or resistance often arises within ourselves, and we will see with better clarity what parts of ourselves are being challenged.

Once we have worked through challenges, we can feel comfortable with another person and can say that we are truly "engaged." Once engaged, it's a matter of choice whether or not to celebrate the experience. This is often referred to as an engagement party and/or marriage ceremony. Regardless of any official celebrations, we will have discovered a soulmate and we can look forward to wonderful experiences and possibilities!

Sex is a very close, personal interaction. In the truest sense of the word, sex can be seen as the core or soul of each individual attempting to fully connect on the physical level to create more life. There are many questions that one could ask of themselves, but two wise questions are:

- *Would we like this experience to be filled with increased ease, pleasure, and anticipation?*

- *Can we accept the possibility of creating dis-ease for immediate gratification?*

When both persons feel comfortable and engaged, this is the best time to take the relationship to a higher and deeper level. Sex in this expanded state creates a life filled with ease and renewal, is life giving, is life creating, and is the true meaning of safe sex.

Sex without going through the process of engagement is readily available. Self-discovery often dictates the "toe in the water" syndrome, so at the very least, it is wise to keep in mind that, sex without regard to being engaged (*inside and out*) can open a door to the world of depletion. In the world of depletion, extreme aspects of lust and lack are often being fueled. The creation of lust is a reflection of too much "attraction" in the mix, and the creation of lack is a reflection of too many "wants" in the mix. Both aspects of lust (*too much stimulation*) and lack (*not enough stimulation*) are destabilizing and unfulfilling. These aspects, left without recognition, usually develop into separations, after periods of disregard. It is wise to reflect on the definition of "regard" (*have relation to or connection with; a respect*) in all relations. Without regard for another, we are either consciously or unconsciously fueling many toxic emotions, including: anger, depression, bitterness, resentment, fear, and anxiety. Disregard is always a lose-lose proposition.

The feelings generated by lust and lack are often confusing as we look for fulfillment and happiness. Extreme scenarios underpinned by lust and lack are often being promoted and accepted in the world media. *As they say in advertising, "sex sells," but by using sexual attraction to sell products, are we blurring the lines between lust and love? Is being in lust often being confused with being in love? Is lust becoming one of the most dangerous drugs in existence today, because of our lack of self-awareness and understanding?*

The more charm is brought to bear, the more potent the strain on our energetic systems. What makes it most dangerous is that people (*often women who lack a solid sense of self*) do not realize what they are participating in until they are well on their way. If sexual interaction develops into an addiction, it is an addiction to another person. The effect of this addiction invariably becomes all consuming and interferes with our inner core. Like excess use of drugs, it takes us away from core-focused living and love, increasing imbalance in life itself.

Over time, if the process of engagement is not being consciously pursued, attraction and chemistry can turn into the destructive drug of lust, rather than becoming a soulmate connection. The chemistry being created by the two individuals reduces the flow of the core and creates imbalances and blockages through lack of attention. The chemistry will be made up of too much personality and physical attraction, and not enough soul connection or self-awareness. When the personality and physical attraction is paramount (*on an ongoing basis*) our ego, our shallower self, is running the show. To "sustain" this chemistry, the ego relies on manipulation, or in other words, control.

I believe that it is useful to be aware of some characteristics of lust in order to become more aware of the characteristics of love. The following brief scenario is a reflection of the "world of lust." You may have experienced this to some degree or have observed similar scenarios.

Jane who is on the receiving end of ego-based attention may feel slightly uncomfortable, but may not understand why. All Jane knows is that this attention may be nothing like she has ever experienced before, it feels really good, and it feels like love. As time goes on, however, this chemistry takes on an increased level of ego versus a soul or core connection, and it feels less and less fulfilling for all concerned. It begins to feel less like love, and it becomes less desirable.

John who is offering this ego-driven attention begins to see the destabilizing effect that it is having on Jane, and he begins to see Jane as weak and less worthy of his attention. The ego never wants to take its share of the responsibility of creating this situation, so the ego often takes a large step back, usually without regard for the other person.

Having the attention withdrawn, Jane may try to change (*adapt*) to please John—in an attempt to regain the sense of connection, desirability, and chemistry. But in trying to adapt, Jane damages her sense of self and loses a piece of her personal integrity in the process. She is no longer being completely true to herself. There are generally internal warning signals at this point that are being ignored.

John/ego is now feeling less stimulated and less satisfied, because the ego is always looking for stimulation outside of itself. Jane, who is no longer receiving the attention, is becoming more insecure and less stimulating to John. If this pattern continues, the ego personality will move on to "greener pastures," and Jane, the original object of the attention, may feel quite lost. During this debilitating process, both may be craving the initial chemistry or verve. This feeling, however, never replicates itself in this energy depleting environment.

Lust needs to be acknowledged and taken seriously. It is highly addictive and depleting, as are most drugs. Often, one or both persons continue to want to partake in what is left of these "relationships" and will try to gain the initial high or verve, even if there is very little left of themselves.

If we are self-aware enough to realize that we are choosing casual sex for physical pleasure, then the odds of addiction go down markedly. The focus will naturally shift more toward the physical, which limits the effect on the person, as a whole. One major issue with this choice is that both parties must understand and agree to the ground rules ahead of time. This conscious acknowledgment and agreement are often considered unromantic and can become a turn off, so the rules are often bypassed. The key is that both parties know what they are engaging in from the beginning. Many people desire casual sex and a whole variety of stimulants. Others find casual sex to be an empty experience at best. *Is the extent of casual sex a reflection of individual self-awareness as a whole? As more people become core-focused and self-aware, will casual sex become less common naturally because it pales in comparison to the "real thing" and the rewards that are available?*

There are many experiences in life that are not considered to be safe. Sex based on personality and physical attraction is, for the most part, far from what one would consider to be safe. We can consciously weigh the risks beforehand only if we are truly self-aware. Self-awareness is the key, and if we know ourselves, this casual option naturally loses a lot of its appeal. If we are looking for ways to experience life and to grow, we might naturally desire this experience in order to learn a thing or two, but it often won't be easy. This experience may attract the "school of hard knocks."

The process of engagement within our romantic relationships has been the primary focus of this chapter, but this process can be used in modified ways within our other close relationships. These relationships often include other family members, friends, co-workers, colleagues, business associates, teammates, or anyone else we have a significant involvement with on a regular basis. Self-awareness, and the maintenance of the integrity of all concerned, creates the ease that we are all looking for, both consciously and unconsciously. "Agreeing to disagree" often creates the space that is required, and "meeting in the middle" creates ease, growth, and expansion, which supports the sustainability of these relationships.

> *"Coming together is a beginning; keeping together is progress; working together is success."*
>
> Anonymous

If uncomfortable feelings arise as a result of any of our close interactions, additional space is needed to allow for the process of engagement, growth, change, and the unfolding. As the process of unfolding takes place, it is wise to realize that our limits are being tested and/or expanded. We need to remain calm, exercise caution, and express our personal truths with a focus on solutions to have a successful outcome for all concerned. Realizing that we all have limits is a sign of maturity. It takes great personal strength and depth of character to hold and tolerate the energy of another in certain circumstances. Losing our balance or our connection to our center and turning to control techniques is something we need to guard against at all times.

It is through the understanding of our differences that we may come together.

BEAUTY OF CHILDREN

One of the most important things that we can do for ourselves
and for children is to allow children to be themselves. In doing
so, children REMAIN connected to their core within and we, in turn,
get brought back closer to our own.

E ngaging in core-focused renewal and living is invaluable to
children. Children arrive in our world with their inner cores
intact, and they are full of hope and vibrant life force energy.
Patterns of thought and behavior play minor roles in their systems
for quite some time. They naturally listen to their inner voice for
guidance and are connected to the core of their being. Consider
how many times you have heard the expressions:

"I love how children are so real."

"If you could bottle their energy and sell it, you would be rich."

"Out of the mouths of babes."

We can learn much about core-focused living from children. It comes so naturally to them. As we learn to become an observer and a guide of children, we learn to read their cues. These cues represent an opportunity for us to change our own thought and behavioral patterns. Children are gifts full of love, curiosity, hopefulness, anticipation, and free-flowing life force energy. Children help us to fully engage the core of our being on a moment-to-moment basis. They are uplifting and priceless. Attuning yourself to children is a life-giving experience for all concerned.

> *"The secret of genius is to carry the spirit of*
> *childhood into maturity."*
>
> Thomas Huxley (1825-1895), an English biologist

It is a common pattern among adults to underestimate the innate wisdom of children. Children are attuned to solid core values as they are still very connected to the energy of their core, which is infused with a knowing of these values. I have spoken to many children under the age of ten who understand the concept of "patterns of behavior" in relation to core values. I have discovered, over the years, that they are very aware of and attuned to the language of energy.

As an example, if a child is hitting other children, many adults may tell the child to stop immediately, scold the child or use well-intentioned control techniques to change his or her behavior. This, however, begins the process of disempowerment and contraction. It is not often considered to simply discuss with or ask the child if she/he understands that hitting is unacceptable, dangerous, and disrespectful, and that hitting is an invasion of personal space. I have discovered, through experience, that the concept of respecting personal space has always been highly understood by children. Once the groundwork has been laid for the consciousness of certain behaviors, then children will focus on changing patterns of behavior that are unacceptable and disrespectful to others and themselves.

Mentioning that these behaviors are merely patterns, and are not a reflection of how wonderful they are as a person is empowering. We all need to feel confident, safe, and secure before we can work through and clear behavioral patterns that do not serve us. Children are then able to separate themselves from a specific "pattern of behavior," and can work on consciously altering the behavior until it is gone. Achieving good outcomes is also very empowering and establishes the ability to take responsibility for their own actions and to feel self-assured.

I have observed that children respond naturally and accept this process. The children that exhibit many challenging patterns of behavior seem especially ready and willing to accept and engage in the process. It has been my observation that these children are particularly bright and are remarkably aware of the effect they are having on others. They are indeed challenging, but they are also looking for ways to be challenged.

"The mind is not a vessel to be filled, but a fire to be kindled."

Plutarch (46ce-119ce), a Greek-Roman biographer and essayist

When we focus on "challenging" behaviors of children as patterns, take a step back, and give space to allow for the unfolding to occur, we will automatically work to shift our own pattern of trying to control the behavior of others. Control patterns can be seen as attempts to force or manipulate others to be or act in a certain way in the present moment. Through observation and support, we help children discover and embody who they truly are deep down inside. When we are supportive of their own inner guidance system, we support our own inner guidance system as well. This creates a win-win situation every time. The change in outcomes may move along at a slower pace than we may be used to, but the resulting changes will be sound, authentic, sustainable, and expansive (*growth orientated*).

The *Back to the Core Within Guidance Cards,* one of the four tools of *The Core-Focused Renewal System,* is a valuable tool for the process of core-focused renewal and living. They offer daily support for opening to the core perspective, especially when interrelating with children. The following are four examples from the sixty-card deck:

Card thirty-three states the following on the front:

I ask children probing questions with an open mind...

And the following on the back:

I make a point of asking probing questions when children and I are conversing. This allows children to get a deeper understanding of themselves and their own world. I receive all responses with an open mind. I allow their opinions to exist without judgment. In this way, children can hear themselves and gain clarity in each and every moment.

Card forty-seven states the following on the front:

My healthy core maximizes my physical health...

And the following on the back:

I acknowledge that my healthy core has a large ripple effect on my entire physical body. As the life force energy flows through my core, it enters all of my cells and acts to rejuvenate and clear my system of toxins that my body absorbs on a daily basis. I also realize that moments of stillness and deep breathing helps the life force energy to flow.

Card thirteen states the following on the front:

As children remain connected to their core, it brings me closer to mine...

<u>And the following on the back:</u>

I realize that as the children in my life remain connected to their core, it brings me back closer to mine. In all decisions that involve them, I look for their reaction to see how it "feels" to them. If I notice resistance, I ask them how they are feeling with an open mind and without judgment. I learn to adjust my decision so that I have agreement. I then breathe deeply within my own system and know that a shift has occurred bringing me closer to my own core.

Card twenty-four states the following on the front:

As I help children find their place in the world, I find my own...

<u>And the following on the back:</u>

As I help children to understand and believe in themselves, I develop a deeper understanding of myself in the process. I remain open and willing to change how I see my world and shed my preconceived notions that no longer serve me. I become more and more authentic, flexible, and youthful as I help children discover themselves.

The intention of the guidance cards is to provide daily affirmations to encourage and inspire us to connect with the wealth of "knowingness" that lies at our core. This connection brings abundance into our daily lives, including: energy, a sense of personal well-being, clarity, balance, growth, and power. Above all, the connection brings a sense of great joy, an appreciation for children, and a deeper connection to life itself. As we draw support from the guidance cards, we reconnect with the "knowingness" that lies at our core. As we allow more "feeling" into our lives, we will soon rediscover that we are much more than what we "think" we are.

The earlier we engage with core-focused renewal and living, the more ease we will experience. As we participate in this process ourselves, it allows the children in our lives to become consciously aware of and to sustain their internal processes as well. Children emulate what they are observing, and as we grow in our ability to be love, so do they.

Believing in children allows us to believe in ourselves. Giving space to children gives space to ourselves. Giving time to children gives time to ourselves. Be a blessing to children, and they will be a blessing to us.

From the perspective of the core, everything in matter is always moving towards balance, and the Law of Engagement is at work to ensure this balance. This overall seeking of balance is reflected at many levels and includes systems of all kinds. If a system is operating in resistance to the Law of Engagement (*which is moving towards balance*), this will be reflected in how much ease or dis-ease there is in the system.

With this perspective in mind, it is useful to contemplate the origins of the word educate. Educate is derived from the Latin word "educo," meaning to educe, to draw out, to develop from within. The term "to draw out" implies that there is latent potential within each person. *Can we conclude that a balanced approach within an educational system is to not only teach general or specialized facts or information, but to develop knowledge within and from each individual?* In other words, to help learners understand and "digest" concepts, motivate children to retain new information, and at the same time, ask what it means to them.

We all process information differently, and it is very important to discover our own process. For example, after a math lesson, a naturally logical child might process this information and begin to develop an interest in engineering and how buildings are constructed. A naturally insightful child might process this lesson and develop an interest in numerology and the relationships between numbers and events. Educating with these differences in mind develops not only the intellectual capacity of children, but also self-awareness, and ultimately, knowledge and motivation.

Self-discovery is of utmost importance to the balance, health, and well-being of the individual, as well as society as a whole. As our societies continue to move closer towards balance and become increasingly aware of the importance of introspection and self-discovery for teaching and learning, a growing number of teaching styles will manifest, or be created naturally.

It is in the best interests of all concerned that we learn to see situations through the eyes of children, especially those children who are struggling in a program or system. Children that are struggling need more of our wisdom, attention, and consideration—not less. The health and well-being of our children and their education always needs to be kept in perspective and moving towards balance.

In terms of core-focused renewal and living, education of any kind is valuable. It stimulates the Fire Element of the Solar Plexus and the Fire oval of the brain. It stimulates self-confidence and the feeling of "I can." It stimulates strength and action and personal power. If there is a desire to be a professional, then much education is required.

It is wise to keep in mind that the Fire Element will be amplified through thought and study. To remain in balance—energetically—we will need to develop other aspects of ourselves as well. We are much more than our thoughts. In fact, the more we enjoy the concept of thinking, the more we will need to connect with core-focused renewal and living to be in balance. *The intellect will become highly developed, but will it be insightful?* An unbalanced lifestyle can manifest as weight gain, high blood pressure, and diabetes (*for example*). A well-developed intellect combined with depth perception or extrasensory perception and a sound body can accomplish much.

We continue to create systems and patterns of eating in the "modern world." *Are these systems and patterns creating ease or dis-ease?* From the perspective of the core, everything in matter is always moving towards balance, so the natural state of being for children is to eat when they are hungry and to stop eating as soon as they begin to feel full. The more children exercise, the more they will "earn" their hunger, and the more they will be able to eat. The healthiest and purest of food is the best to eat, along with ample water. The earlier we establish this pattern of balance, the easier it is to maintain, the more natural it feels, and the larger the stabilizing effect on our body in the long run.

We often find ourselves eating for reasons other than hunger, such as for emotional reasons. As children observe our behavior, they will develop similar patterns. Chronic eating of this kind is eating with dis-ease in mind. In other words, we are fueling a pattern of behavior that will create dis-ease within our system. Over time, chronic patterns manifest or materialize as physical problems or disease. The level of our physical discomfort will be in direct relation to our level of resistance to the Law of Engagement, which is always moving us towards inner balance.

When we overeat, or eat for any reason other than hunger, we are disengaging from the supportive energy of our Root Chakra and our Earth Element. We are also disconnecting from our Base Vortex and the supportive source energy of our Earth Mother and her bounty, in favor of connecting with our patterns of thought and behavior that are not serving us. An imbalance is being fuelled.

In the modern world, many addictive foods and comforts of the "easy lifestyle" have been created. Although advertised as creating ease or creations for ease, there is a clear path to disease (*dis-ease*) that has developed and continues to grow. Unfortunately, many very addictive foods are designed for and targeted at children. As most of us are well aware, it is very hard to break any addictions, especially those that are unconsciously developed in childhood.

Chronic malnutrition, or the lack of proper nutrition over time also has negative long-term consequences, as does food scarcity. Malnutrition is most concerning, as it is much harder to recognise in ourselves and in children in our immediate day-to-day lives.

The focus of addictive foods is short term gains for long term pains. As more of us choose core-focused renewal, poor nutrition and over-consumption at the expense of our health and well-being will be reduced. The key is to continue to plant the seeds of awareness—every time we eat for any reason other than hunger, or eat low-quality food, or more than we are burning off through exercise, we are eating in a dis-eased way. We are consciously supporting and fueling an imbalance within our system. This imbalance will be met with the powerful energy of the Law of Engagement, which is always seeking balance on our behalf. How this imbalance will manifest in our lives is out of our control. What is within our control is the power of conscious choice.

SELF-REFLECTION AND SELF-DISCOVERY

Self-reflection and self-discovery—a practice and a purpose worthy of our time and deepest commitment.

"This above all: to thine own self be true,
And it must follow, as the night the day,
Thou canst not be false to any man.
Farewell, my blessing, season this in thee!"

William Shakespeare, Hamlet, Act 1, Scene III (Polonius)

The self or soul or core of our being is very strong, because it is infused with a knowing of solid core values. To be true to ourselves is to be true to our soul and our solid core values. This becomes clearer, the more we self-reflect and discover who we truly are deep down inside. If we are being true to ourselves, we cannot be false to any person. If we try to be false, we will be going against ourselves, and we will feel it. *As we become consciously*

*aware of this fact, why would we want to drain and deplete our-
selves? There would be nothing to gain and everything to lose!*

The concept of developing deeper self-awareness, or discover-
ing the world of "hidden knowledge," is reflected in temples and
sacred sites all over the world. Temples are offering messages by
their basic structures. As we begin to expand our awareness of
this "hidden" world, we are able to see the messages that are being
offered with more clarity. Messages that are being offered reinforce
the gravity of being true to ourselves and developing our inner
knowing and energy awareness. As we deepen our self-awareness,
we support growth and expansion within, which results in a
broader connection to source energy (*the infinite*) that is flowing
through us and surrounding us.

Consciously increasing our self-awareness and connecting to
"all that is" is very exhilarating and can begin at any moment. We
need to ask ourselves this question:

*How much love (how much of ourselves) do we put into what
we do?*

We need to know ourselves before we can pour ourselves into
anything. It is not how much we give, but how much love we put
into giving. As we are "being love" we are deepening our capacity
to do from this place of knowing.

We all have needs. Our wants are many. Our basic needs, both
physically and energetically, as authentic human beings can be
seen as surroundings for shelter, air for breath, fire for warmth,
water for hydration, and earth for nourishment; the elements
more subtly are Ether Element for personal space, Air Element
for heartfelt feelings, Fire Element for thought and action, Water
Element for flow and feeling deeply, Earth Element for support
and grounding. Getting even subtler, the Crown Chakra/vortex
for connection to Source (*the divine masculine for insights that
allow us to think "outside the box"*), Brow Center for insightful
thought, Base Vortex for connection to Source (*the divine feminine*

for support, accepting, and "believing in the present moment," and in the unfolding). We also need the Law of Engagement—it helps us to feel our way towards balance in each and every moment— as well as the Law of Attraction—it helps us to realize our focus by what we are manifesting in our surroundings.

Our true nature is one of goodness. Expansive life force energy naturally flows with ease through our core, and all of our major energy spheres. All energies are equally important to our health and well-being, and our ability to be renewed and to manifest our desires in our lives. There are a multitude of characteristics that describe these energy spheres and are beyond the scope of this book. The *Back to the Basics Guide to Energy Awareness*, one of the four tools of *The Core-Focused Renewal System*, offers descriptions of many of these characteristics and amplifiers. The more we get to know our subtle energy body, the easier and more automatic it becomes to engage our core selves, supporting us at deeper levels on a regular basis.

Balance is the key, and the Law of Engagement prompts us at all times, without exception, to help us to keep moving towards balance. If we take a step back as an individual, we begin to see that the Law of Engagement is working at all times on a grand scale. You may have heard of the concept that we are all one "in the grand scheme of things." Usually this concept meets with resistance as it seems too far-fetched and perplexing. What happens globally, however, is a direct reflection of our collective balance or imbalance. The amount of personality, or "ego" reaction, is reflected in the level of conflict and lack that exists, whereas the amount of "core" response is reflected in the level of ease and vibrancy that exists.

Due to the conflict and lack in existence in the world today, we can see that a great number of us are still living from the more personal, shallower perspective of the personality or ego. This is not a reflection of our expansive and true human natures. This merely tells us what we do not know about ourselves yet. We are always, and will always be, "works in progress," in the effort to connect more fully to our true human nature and our authentic selves.

Freedom to choose introspection to discover our true multidimensional natures and our individuality is the key to core-focused renewal and living. The key is choice. Choice brings about true freedom and is needed in order to expand our state of being.

I ask for guidance and insights from the higher powers, or God, and I know that the messages I receive are always for my highest good, but I also know that I must rely on the energies surrounding me to create my world. Like the theme "In God we trust." I find myself saying, "In Mother Earth I trust." Also, I like to say, "In the Source I trust." or "In the Universe I trust."

When we connect to source energy "above and below," we realize that it is through our own thoughts and actions, and our own choices, that we are creating our world around us. To engage our core as much as possible allows for a clearer and stronger connection to source energy and life itself.

Why would you want to do it any other way?

In the short run, it takes focus to shift and change reactive patterns, but in the long run, is there any question?

It is wise to keep reminding ourselves that the Law of Engagement is working within us and around us at all times. To live in resistance to this law is to create dis-ease in our system, our life, and in the lives of those around us, especially those that are closest to us—our loved ones.

One might ask why there are so many people who appear to be disconnected from who they truly are.

If the Law of Engagement exists, how have so many people deviated from their inner core for so long?

Are we supporting the freedom of choice adequately and the consciousness of the effects of choice?

Perhaps the concepts of right timing and society's support of the resistance to the Law of Engagement, through the promotion of drugs and distractions also play roles. In our current reality there appears to be an imbalance of masculine "thinking" energy and feminine "feeling" energy. Men and women embody both energies, but it is women, who are the true feminine, who embody the powerful maternal drive of the world, and they offer the "feeling" energy naturally and in abundance.

The imbalance of the "thinking" and "feeling" energies, as a whole, can be a result of many factors, including: repression (*or bullying*) and a basic lack of consideration for perceived minorities, most specifically women and children. Although this imbalance is decreasing, the frequent disregard of the qualities of the true feminine persists and is damaging and depleting for everyone. The damaging effect is reflected in numerous ways throughout the world. One very obvious manifestation is that many of us lack integrity and authenticity, and we experience much suffering or discomfort and dis-ease in our daily lives. The true feminine or "feeling" energy knows the importance and gravity of nurturing, protecting, and challenging ourselves and our children so that we develop a strong and clear sense of self.

In broader terms, this imbalance is reflected in our lack of respect for, and giving space to, the divine feminine energy of Mother Earth or Gaia, which seeks to support our health and well-being, growth, and expansion.

Why have we continued to overlook the obvious—that we cannot survive without the supportive energy and the messages that emanate from nature?

There are countless messages being offered every day from the natural world. Our Earth Mother is always promoting and supporting our health, well-being, growth, and expansion.

The vastness of the sky and the solar system speaks of the importance of personal space and our multidimensional natures.

The winds that blow through reflect the power of our breath, our touch, our words, and the effect they can have on others.

The fires that burn reflect the power of our thoughts and actions. They can both destroy and renew.

The constant movement of water reflects the power of our deep feelings and emotions and the ebb and flow of life.

The ground, the earth that supports and nurtures us all, reflects the importance of a healthy physical body to support and sustain our lives.

A core perspective lets us realize that if we live in resistance to our true selves, increased dis-ease will be a result. What materializes or manifests to combat or fight dis-ease will most often be a product of logic and thought. Our brain has immense capabilities that are being proven every day. There is much dis-ease in the world and many medical breakthroughs as a result.

If, however, we become attuned to the Law of Engagement, and connect with the feminine energy of introspection and self-reflection, we will see the parts of ourselves that are out of balance and bring ourselves closer to center/balance, and closer to ease. We would also be bringing the feminine "feeling" and masculine "thinking" energies closer to balance.

Core-focused renewal and living is a process and is perfect in its imperfection. The imperfection allows for constant stimulation, or stirring, which is a requirement of change and growth. Sometimes it feels uncomfortable, and at other times it feels unbearable, but just like any storm, these feelings pass and openings are created for renewal and for something new to develop. Newness is born.

> *"It is not light that we need, but fire; it is not the gentle shower, but thunder. We need the storm, the whirlwind, and the earthquake."*
>
> Frederick Douglass (1818-1895), an African-American social reformer, orator, writer and statesman

Is there a fear that the growth of individuality will cause chaos or major disruptions in our societal systems currently in place?

This pattern of thought thinks that individuality, or the freedom to choose what resonates (*feels right*) to ourselves will be destructive to society as a whole. If we focus on being true to ourselves and engaging our inner core, however, we will attune to our inner voice. This voice is always coming from our higher self, which only truly acknowledges and understands solid core values in everyday life. Being true to ourselves allows us to connect with and embody our higher self through the process, and in doing so we create expansion, renewal, and more of all that is good. There is nothing to fear and everything to gain.

The core of our being is very respectful of what is, and so our societal systems/structures will go through renewal over time. There will not be destruction as we see it today—this is merely a reflection of the disrespect or disregard of what is and what has come before us.

Many of us still try to be something or somebody we are not. This is often because we lack self-awareness. We have all worked very hard to create an easier lifestyle for many. One of the problems with this development is that many of us are able to go through life with "blinders" on and still "survive". We can pretend to be someone that we believe is more appealing to others, or be someone that we have been told to be. The result is that we never really develop a true sense of self and depth perception (*to perceive from deepening levels within*).

A major problem arises with this lifestyle when significant pressure eventually enters our lives—generally through the Law of Engagement, seeking balance on our behalf. Many of us choose resistance through drugs, alcohol, suffering, and dis-ease rather than consciously working through pressure situations so that we can grow toward increased inner balance.

This dynamic of resistance could never exist in nature. When the storm hits, the focus is on survival, and this is the accepted norm. Resistance to engagement and balance undermines our ability to adapt and survive on our own when pressure situations arise (*when the storm hits*).

As an analogy of nature and society: I was sitting on my lanai (*covered terrace*), writing in my notebook, in Molokai. Molokai is considered to be the "most Hawaiian" of all the islands in the archipelago. To me, Molokai reflects the "deep life" in abundance. As I was enjoying the beautiful views all around me, a storm blew in very quickly, and I observed how the palm trees were responding.

When the storm hits and the palm trees are swaying, do the trees blame the storm for making them feel vulnerable?

No. They hope that they are strong and flexible enough to endure the pressure of the storm. The tree relies on all of its parts and is fully engaged in survival. The coconuts that are already ripe let go, reducing weight at the top. Any branches that are no longer viable are released to the ground, and the roots seek depth in order to hold on. The trunk is grateful for its natural curve that is positioned to move with the wind. The tree holds on, engages all of its parts, and endures. After the storm has passed, which the tree knows it will, it will actually feel lighter, stronger and renewed, grateful for the storm knowing that all is well.

We can learn so much from observing nature. As we watch a palm tree sway in a storm, we can see how it is fully engaged in maintaining its integrity and surviving. We can see the importance of being in the right place at the right time, to be authentic.

> *"The whole secret of the study of nature lies*
> *in the learning how to use one's eyes."*
>
> George Sand (1804-1876), French novelist, memoirist and socialist

To maintain our authenticity, we need to learn how to consciously engage ourselves and our inner core, especially when involved in pressure situations. We need to embrace, enjoy, and own our uniqueness, and respect the uniqueness of others. We need to learn how to consciously engage our major energy spheres, connect to source energy for insights and support, and seek balance within.

If we have been focused on trying to be someone else, or pretending to be somebody we are not, this consciousness will be beyond our reach in the present moment. When pressure situations arise, our coping mechanisms will be weak, and the resulting manifestations may not be very pleasant.

There are many manmade institutions that have been established to control, limit, or govern our behavior. We have created many laws, and a large court and jail system that, in actuality, is supporting the resistance to the Law of Engagement. The Law of Engagement presents itself as imperfect, as it responds in accordance to the freedom to choose our focus.

As we are aware, by the extensiveness of the legal system and incarcerations, there are many of us that continue to ignore, or to be distracted from, the subtle urgings to remain engaged in a balanced way, instead (*consciously or unconsciously*) experiencing the "School of Hard Knocks" and suffering. As our resistance to this natural law decreases, along with the increase in our consciousness of this law and its effects, our relative ease will increase. As a result, there will be less need for manmade laws and institutions. This will be reflected in fewer laws and more streamlined court and jail systems.

*"My concern is not whether God is on our side; my greatest
concern is to be on God's side, for God is always right.
When I do good, I feel good. When I do bad, I feel bad.
That's my religion."*

Abraham Lincoln, 16th President of the United States,
Senatorial Speech, USA, 1858

We have also developed a large medical system to support health, improve the quality of life, and extend our expected life span. To a great extent, however, this system has been created to combat dis-ease. As less resistance to engagement and self-reflection is attained, this will be reflected in a more streamlined medical system and pharmaceutical industry. There will be more ease and less dis-ease.

We have also created a large military establishment to protect the peace, but it is also designed to engage in war. The focus on war will decrease as more ease is created in individuals. The military establishment will be able to focus more on peace keeping, natural disaster relief, and providing aid.

Sometimes the resistance to any kind of change will be the thought of loss of employment, or a perceived change in the power structure. This change, however, will be relatively slow, steady, and respectful, as it will only come about through engaging solid core values and experiencing increased ease and vibrancy levels in everyday life. Any changes will be naturally balanced and expansive as the gains of "the renewed" will far offset any perceived losses of the "old."

If we have unconsciously or consciously deviated from our core, or from being true to ourselves, or being introspective in pressure situations, we just need to choose to re-engage with our core in the next pressure situation. Increasing and renewing the flow of our life force energy is available and abundant to all, available at any moment—this is intended to be second nature.

If we find ourselves in circumstances that are compromising our integrity, then we will know that we need to self-reflect and decide to make alteration, or face the depletion of our authentic self, and our true individuality. We will also be unconsciously or consciously "calling" the "force to be reckoned with" (*the energy of the Law of Engagement*) to make itself more apparent to us. To learn how to attune to our needs in the present moment is the key. To understand that how we are feeling about ourselves and others is our indicator of our alignment or misalignment to our core in the present moment.

> *"We are unable to grow toward greater understanding.*
> *of our true nature unless we take the time to examine.*
> *and reflect upon our life."*

Socrates (c470BC-c399BC), a classical Greek philosopher

CORE-FOCUSED
RENEWAL

There are many opportunities for energy renewal in everyday life,
if our choices are core-focused in a balanced way.

Experiencing energy renewal and energy depletion

Example One—Asking:

"Ask and it is given."

Given that we need to move towards greater balance, ease, and
vibrancy, I asked Source to help me be able to write this book and
to express my truths with relative ease. Every time that I tried to
write in the past, I became blocked. It became a struggle. For some
reason, I always forget that I will be given what I need to align
with a desire to have it fulfilled. After I asked for any blockages to
clear, I found myself going through some incredibly challenging

pressure situations that facilitated the alignment necessary to have my thoughts flow with greater ease.

After twenty years, you would think I would be bracing myself, but no. I always remember the outcomes, and these are always for my highest good, so I keep asking, receiving, and growing. I see the asking as being similar to the desire for children. After giving birth and experiencing the labor involved, you would think that one would never want to go through that experience again. However, the gift of our baby is so worth the effort that we usually forget all about the challenges until the moment that we are laboring once again.

Observing the animated (*being full of energy and life*) natural world of Molokai as I wrote in my notebook, I was compelled to compare my asking to that of a palm tree wishing or sending out a signal to the universe to be relieved of some of its ripe coconuts. After the asking, a gale force wind hits it during the night. So comes the saying, "Be careful what you wish for!"

Example Two—Unfolding:

We can choose to learn great lessons and experience the energy of renewal even with the simplest of requests. We ask for a sunny day, for example. We wake up and it is still raining—it is so tempting to complain. The vibration of complaining, however, is heavy and toxic and creates energy blocks (*dense matter*) and tension within our system.

To be in appreciation, we could say to ourselves, *At least the rain makes everything green. When the sun comes out, all of the plants will be ready for the heat. Thank you for the rain.*

With this process in mind, we will have given ourselves an uplifting feeling, almost as if the sun really had come out. We are also transmitting the message to the universe that we are in appreciation and acceptance of the present moment. We trust and have faith that all is well in our world and that the sun will come out when the timing is right.

Repetition—daily practice—is a very important part of the process. Repetition creates a stronger desire, and our strong and clear desire—our vibrancy level—sends a clear signal to the universe that we are alive and well and open for all that is good.

Our next request is filled with a stronger desire. *Please provide me with a sunny day; the sun makes me feel so happy!* The rain keeps coming. Even though it is so tempting to be angry and frustrated, we keep looking for the good in all things. *The garden looks so beautiful in the rain. Look at the ducks and how they enjoy the rain. The rain has such a cleansing effect on everything. The sun will break through one of these days!*

Our energy is still being uplifted, flowing, and we are creating enrichment within ourselves. The rain keeps coming. Our desire continues to grow. After many, many, many days of rain, we just give into the rain and accept it. The next day, the sun shines brightly, and we almost miss seeing the rain, but we love the sun and give thanks and enjoy each moment.

Did we really need the sun, or did we just need to learn patience, acceptance, and appreciation of "all that is" while staying in a state of joy and happiness?

To remain open to receive our wishes and desires, we need to walk in joy and happiness. This does take conscious effort, especially at first, but it can become second nature, especially as we see the rewards. Consciously focusing on the feelings of joy and happiness, is like opening up a line of communication between ourselves and the animated (*lively, vigorous; having life*) material/natural world. It gives us the power to manifest what we need to be happy and for our highest good.

To know what we currently want is one thing; to know and be open to what we truly need is another. Our true needs, which are in the process of expansion, always remain just beyond our current comprehension or understanding. This keeps our connection to source energy alive and tests our trust and faith in the unfolding. The strength of this trust and faith grows over time, as we see our lives unfolding in ways that are always for our highest good and our highest state of joy.

<u>Example Three—Disbelief:</u>

To depict the true power of appreciation in action, we can take a look at an opposite approach of anger and judgment to see an example of energy depletion. We ask for a sunny day because we are sick of the rain. *I want a sunny day!* The next morning it is raining. *"Rain again! I thought if I asked, it would be given!"*

Later that evening, we ask again with a smile and a friendlier tone of voice. *Please send me a sunny day.* Next morning it is pouring! *"I can't go to work in this crap! There is no way that I am getting on the bus!"*

We are, in effect, creating tension within and causing our energy flow to slow down, and even to get blocked. We are creating a lower vibrancy level within our system. We are putting a great deal of pressure on ourselves, and we will feel even more tired and depressed and less at ease.

"I think that I am getting sick!"

We wake up to more rain. Our cold feels worse. We can't make it into work, and we call in sick. During the day, we think about all of the other things in our life that are not working. We feel worse, and we shut ourselves off from receiving anything worthwhile or inspired. The flow of our energy body slows down, and we are overshadowing (*clouding over*) our inner core with dense matter created by our patterns of negative thought. We find ourselves thinking, *"This 'ask and it is given' crap, doesn't work!"*

The next day the sun shines brightly, but we can't enjoy it because we are too sick to get out of bed. We now have another wish—we wish those kids next door would be quiet. Their loud voices of enjoyment are making our head pound! We don't believe in the process of the "Great Mystery" anymore, so we get up and yell at the children to be quiet. We decide that to attempt to control others is a much better way to go.

The more consciously joyful we become, the easier it is to remain in a joyful state. It takes effort to dissipate/clear blocks, in order to leave behind patterns of thought and behavior that no longer serve us. As we continue to engage our inner core, we embody more of who we truly are, we become more authentic in nature, and everything takes on greater ease, including having our desires manifest.

Example Four—Process of Engagement:

Having had enough of one-night stands and unfulfilling relationships, Susan is ready to try this process of engagement with the very handsome man she met last night. Susan knows that the physical attraction is there, and he makes her laugh all of the time. These characteristics definitely meet her wants. Susan agrees to go out on a date to see where this takes her. She had a good dinner, full of laughs and chemistry, and then he suggests that they go to his place for dessert. Instead of dessert, Susan talks about the process of engagement and her desire to experience the expansiveness and ease of a soul connection over time. Pleasantly surprised, he says that he will respect her desire and is keen to learn more about this connection and process. They mutually decide to meet again for a walk so that they can get to know each other better. Susan feels a sense of relief, joy, and the expansiveness at the thought of a new approach, rather than going down the same old fast lane and expecting a different outcome. She begins to feel a sense of renewal, an uplifting sense of knowing that she is on the right track. She believes that these senses are enough to sustain her in the present moment.

Example Five—World of Lust:

Susan has had enough of one-night stands and has recently met a very handsome man. She knows that the physical attraction level is high. This characteristic definitely meets her wants. She has agreed to go out on a date to see where this takes her. They had a good dinner full of laughs and chemistry and then he suggests that they go to his place for dessert. First, Susan talks about the process of engagement and her desire to experience the expansiveness and ease of a soul connection over time.

Susan is met with the controlling/manipulating energy of the ego. Instead of an agreement to seek a soul connection, he looks deeply into her eyes, and says *"Are you sure you aren't interested in some dessert?"* She feels her resolve to experience something new and expansive begin to weaken. She makes the choice to throw caution to the wind just one more time—she hopes that this time it will be different.

As the weeks go by with diminishing exchanges, she is now kicking herself for expecting a different outcome. She acknowledges the feelings of discomfort that have manifested within. This pattern of behavior does not support her inner balance, and definitely no longer serves her.

Responding versus reacting and the process of freeing our spirit to dig a little deeper

Example One—Parenting:

Our teenager crashed our car last night. No one got hurt, but the car is a write-off. We react by wielding our anger at our teenager by making grounding rules and throwing out harsh words. We end up creating more tension and stress and a decrease in the flow of life force energy within all concerned. We also create fear—fear of more consequences, as one can just imagine. This reaction doesn't change the fact that the car is a write-off.

Responding from our inner core or higher self, most specifically from the sphere of our heart, would not change the situation, but it would allow for something more loving to develop. The situation will become a learning experience for everyone involved, and everyone will develop more self-awareness. Pressure situations of all kinds can be looked upon as growth opportunities.

Our response includes some swearing, but not directed at anyone—just at the situation. We ask questions with an open mind and consider anything our teen wants to tell us. We want what is best for our teen, after all—this is guaranteed!

When we ask questions, we all naturally self-reflect. Adding in our own past "mistakes" that were similar continues to soften the situation.

It is truly amazing how this approach creates inward reflection for everyone, and naturally, the outcomes always include growth and renewal. The car is still smashed, but the situation has become a learning and renewing experience, without added fear and without creating separation. More love energy has been created out of a challenging and pressure-filled experience.

A common response that helps to ease the way is, *"It could always be worse."* Our teenagers will naturally become more careful in the future, and they will begin to feel the full gravity of the situation rather than wasting energy rebelling against the angry reactions of their parents. The weight of taking on the responsibility of a mistake is not soon forgotten and is often life altering.

Example Two—Sexuality and Sexiness:

Sex and sexiness are often used to control others and to control situations. It is also used to sell products of all kinds. The misunderstandings and illusions of sex and sexiness are many. The following are some example responses that could be used to help increase self-reflection for all and to create ease and more space for something new to develop:

Statement: If you don't have sex with me, that means you don't love me.

Response: *I need to be in love with you first to have sex with you. This could take some time. Have you heard about the process of engagement?*

Statement: I can't have sex with you until we are married.

Response: *What about when we are truly engaged? I bet that you won't consider saying no then.*

Statement: Wow, you are so beautiful. I am so hot for you!

Response: *I am hot for you, too! How do you feel about raising a child?*

Statement: Try this drug. Sex is so incredible when you are on this drug!

Response: *I prefer the thought of soulmate sex. Do you want to see whether we can be soulmates instead?*

Statement: Buy this dress and you will attract all of the men!

Response: *Hey, wait a minute! That model is 5' 10" and 22 years old, and I am 5' 2" and 40. That dress will not look the same on me. Even if it did, would attracting "all of the men" really make me happy?*

Self-reflection, or introspection in the moment, versus judging and reacting *(creating space for renewal and expansion rather than contraction and depletion)*

Example One—With Our Partners

Thought: Boy does my partner ever look fat just sitting there watching sports, yet again.

Response: *I think that I will take off my own sweat pants and put on my tight pair of jeans to keep myself honest. I think that I may find new thoughts and new approaches.*

Thought: Why doesn't my partner ever take out the garbage?

Response: *Thank goodness I don't have to deal with the car.*

Thought: My partner does not turn me on in the slightest anymore.

Response: *I think that I'll put on my bathing suit and see how comfortable I feel in my own skin.*

Example Two—With Our Children

Thought: Why are my teenagers so difficult to communicate with?

Response: *Today I will ask for an opinion from my teenagers and keep an open mind. I may be pleasantly surprised! Maybe I need to get to know their worlds a bit better.*

Thought: Just look at that tattoo on my teenager. It looks like crap!

Response: *I guess my outdated hair style and outdated clothes don't look so hot either.*

Thought: Why doesn't my two-year-old stop running and getting into everything!

Response: *I am so glad that my child is happy and healthy. I better get more rest, eat better, and get more exercise so that I can keep up! Boy what a sacrifice!*

Example Three: With Those Around Us

Thought: Why are other people such rotten drivers?

Response: *I did go too fast in a school zone the other day, rushing to pick up my own kids from another school.*

Thought: The world is such an awful mess!

Response: *Why do I even watch or read the news. I already know that the news reports mainly on the activities of those who are disconnecting from their core and the resulting doom and gloom.*

Thought: Look at that person. They look so happy. They must be having an easy life!

Response: *I know that this is not true. Nobody has it easy in the long run. That thought is just an illusion. I bet that looking happy is one way to ensure a life of more ease and vibrancy for myself.*

Keep your sense of humor—it eases the way. The gift of humor alters the chemistry of any situation. When we laugh at ourselves first and remain amused by our own reactions, we become our own personal alchemist.

evolve

CORE-FOCUSED LIVING

"To be or not to be"—*Is there really any question?*

We all have hopes, dreams, and desires, as long as we remain truly alive. When we ask or pray for something, we are actually sending a signal to the universe to bring us what we need in order to receive what it is that we have asked for. The stronger our inner core, the greater our state of ease and vibrancy and the stronger our signal and our capacity to take on more of what life has to offer.

What manifests in our surroundings might not be exactly what we asked for, but it will be exactly what we need for our highest good—it will be what we need to continue to grow in a balanced way. Asking for something implies that we wish to expand beyond our current level of consciousness. The universal energies are always aligned with growth, expansion, and renewal. They rejoice in the asking, and they respond consistently.

It helps to have the belief that anything is possible, and that each and every one of us has an inner core where source energy flows abundantly, and that a connection to this energy is our natural state of being. It also helps to extend our full respect and understanding toward pressure situations and our possible resistance to make necessary changes. When we are changing our patterns of thought and challenging our behavior, resistance often appears. Change can be very challenging to our system, as it requires that we attune inward and begin the work of dissipating blocks (*dense matter*) that may be very deeply rooted. To help soften our resistance, it is wise to remember that these patterns once served us well and developed for good reason. It's just that their time has passed.

Our primary focus is first to determine if our patterns are creating problems/blocks, and if so, to dissipate/clear them in the present moment, rather than being hard on ourselves and others for allowing them to develop in the first place. When resistance is felt or seen in others, we need to demonstrate acceptance to maintain our own integrity. In practicing acceptance, we will create the space needed to allow for the unfolding to take place for everyone.

When we think that we want something really badly, it is tempting to put pressure on situations through manipulation to get it. This is the controlling energy of the ego working to force an outcome. It is wise to remember, however, that we are all being guided and supported by source energy and the Law of Engagement. As individuals, our only true power is to choose our own response in any given situation. Rather than feeling disappointed or judging certain events and outcomes, focus on acceptance. *Who knows what this acceptance will bring about.* Learn to trust in the unfolding. As we stoke the fire of our desires through self-reflection, our desires grow clearer and stronger. When desires are combined with trust, faith, and inspired action, miracles can happen. This combined force can move mountains!

If we do not ask for much, our connection to the world of renewable source energy will be less obvious. Our world will, more often than not, be small or will narrow rather than expand over time. If we ask for a lot and then resist what is manifesting in our lives, we may get what we asked for over time, but we will suffer and create dis-ease and lack in the process.

If we carefully ask for things that we feel will bring us joy and happiness, then consciously and with appreciation accept what comes to us, we will grow, and create renewal and ease in our world. We will be working towards abundance of all kinds.

If we maintain a core focus and choose to grow through all of our experiences without judgment, we will get glimpses of the expansive world of renewable source energy, one layer or veil at a time. In other words, our true clarity (*seeing things as they truly are, not our opinionated view of how they are*) will be expanding, along with our energetic depth levels. This combination of true clarity and energetic depth develops into depth perception (*to perceive from deepening levels within*) and is also known as extra-sensory perception. Engaging our core in a balanced way amplifies self-love, our higher self, and our connection to Mother Earth's pure love or divine feminine energy. We will realize that we are core-creating (*embodiment of our core as we create*) our reality.

The natural world of which we are a part is beautiful, vibrant, untamed, resilient, colorful, intense, spectacular, full of energy and power, abundant, predictable, unpredictable, bright, dark, sparkling, cold, hot, windy, calm, soft, flowing, accepting...

These attributes and more are reflected in each of us as we engage our core within and uncover our multidimensional natures.

How strongly do you engage your inner core?

What areas in your life are creating relative ease?

What patterns are causing dis-ease, such as over-eating, over-thinking, over-analyzing, over-stressing, over-working, blaming others, and blaming circumstances?

These patterns continue to fuel an unbalanced state or position and contribute to creating an environment in which we are not taking responsibility for our own happiness and well-being. We are, in effect, depleting our own personal power, as well as the personal power of others.

Core-focused living asks that we focus on who we truly are—our true essence—and to maintain our integrity at all times, as this will create a fulfilling and joyful life. It does not matter the level or length of our effect on others. We are all individuals, we are from differing lineages and backgrounds, and we are at different stages in our lives. One person might strive to affect thousands of people, and end up affecting themselves and those closely connected to themselves. Others might strive to help themselves and end up helping the entire world. We are not in control of how things will unfold, we are only responsible for maintaining our own integrity, and respecting the integrity and the space of others.

The Source "above" most closely connected to our thoughts, our brain, sends us many messages continuously. We receive these messages and resulting insights as long as we remain open to them. Insights become more expansive as we develop our inner core and allow for the flow of life force energy to expand. The Source "below" most closely connected to our actions, our physical body, and our feelings and emotions, sends us many messages manifest through how we are feeling and looking in the present moment. These messages flow more readily as we learn to heed them and act accordingly. When we are open to new insights and we act with integrity, we are appreciating, accepting, and allowing source energy to flow, and to connect us with our highest good. We have less resistance to change, and we are in a state of balance and relative ease.

As individuals, we have the power of choice—to choose how to think and act; to choose what to focus on.

Do we wish to bring out the best in ourselves and others, or not?

Do we live in resistance to the Law of Engagement and change, or do we live with appreciation, acceptance, and alignment to the flow of life force energy, no matter how challenging?

Alignment leads us to greater ease, vibrancy, health and well-being, and the experience of being truly alive and living an authentic life. The universe allows for the freedom to choose. The duality within the universe (*light/dark, yin/yang, hot/cold*) gives us the option to choose at all times. If our lives are manifesting large amounts of dis-ease, we will know that we are off-balance or dis-engaging from our core, or our authenticity. We will know that it is time to choose with more personal self-reflection and integrity and "let the chips fall where they may," or in other words, trusting in the unfolding.

The current state of affairs of our world is a reflection of the connection or disconnection to our inner core as a whole. In the broader perspective, we are one energy. It is helpful to know that the news media continues to report on the activities of those who are reacting from their ego and not responding from their core or higher self. It is good to keep in mind that there are many individuals who are making a conscious choice to connect with their core and personal integrity, even though the news continues to report on those who are not.

Is the disconnection from the core becoming more extreme?

Are the extremists in all areas of life actually helping to fuel the desire to find expanded ways of interrelating?

Will more and more people choose authenticity in our quest for more peace, harmony, and goodwill in our own lives, no matter how challenging in the short run?

Often, when we are confronted with a choice, we must take a leap of faith or a step into the unknown. This takes courage. Our levels of true clarity are being challenged in the process and this can feel unsettling and uncertain for a period of time. Rather than choosing this growth and newness, we can become embroiled in anger, violence, force, and power struggles. We can become depleted while looking for answers outside of ourselves, or we can discover solutions by choosing the familiar, yet often untested path of the moving center, engaging our core in a balanced way and experiencing the expansive world of renewable source energy. Our true clarity will experience growth over time as part of this expansion. As new concepts and surroundings come into view, this expanded view is exhilarating, fulfilling, and miraculous.

A centered, deeper path calls for an increased level of self-reflection, self-empowerment, and personal responsibility in our own lives. This path is intended to deepen our self-awareness and to create more peace, harmony, and ease within and without. The path of looking inward and outward in a balanced way is perhaps untested or unproven for many, but known throughout time. Like any exploration, it does require courage and faith to make changes and to stay the course.

If we remain connecting to our desires, open to and truly listening to our inner voice, acting upon the messages that are being delivered, and trusting in the unfolding, we will be supported by our core and source energy. We will be creating abundance in our lives as well as, health, well-being, joy, and happiness. As more individuals choose the path of looking within and without, (*increased introspection*) in their daily lives, this path will naturally become more known, anticipated, accepted, supported, familiar, broader, and less daunting.

Will the extreme actions being undertaken today in an effort to force change (for example, 9/11) be seen as too extreme by all, including the perpetrators? Will the extreme options become distant memories?

Are we beginning to consciously see the great opportunity of self-discovery and renewal on a grand scale? Does this opportunity present itself very often?

Throughout time, there have been, and will continue to be, the few who travel this path, and they often do it alone. Hopefully, in the not-too-distant future, there will be so many people choosing to travel this path, connecting with their inner core, that it will never leave our global consciousness. As individuals, we will remain conscious of the choice to engage our core within and to be supportive of our state of balance, with fuller self-expression in our everyday lives.

Our freedom to choose a balanced connection to our core within is reflected in the depth of our soul, the strength of our physical body, and the clarity of our mind. Our soul, body, and mind—as a balanced unit—allows for the continuous connection to the infinite that is flowing all around us and within us.

The Law of Engagement is always responding on our behalf, providing cues to help us engage our inner core in a balanced way, and allowing us to maintain and sustain a balanced state of being. Balance allows us to grow and connect with our highest good, with relative ease, and to act from this peaceful place of knowing. The extent of our personal growth and development is a choice, as well as a matter of opportunity and timing.

To "be love" is to be fully engaging your core within. Love yourself. Self-love is to believe in yourself, to know yourself, and to be true to yourself. To be in love is to be yourself and to be engaging with the self of another. Life is not meant to be easy, but to be "of ease." To get the most out of life, and to let life get the most out of you, embrace your inner core and engage it as you act.

POSTFACE

A core perspective offers a way to navigate life with greater ease by developing a strong sense of self. By focusing on this perspective, I have been able to guide myself through some very "rough waters," and I have been able to receive much joy in the process. This perspective has also created openings for me to see beyond what I already knew or ever thought it was possible to know. It has been during these moments of true clarity that I have received the greatest feelings of joy and exhilaration, and they have brought the biggest smiles to my face.

My hope in offering my story of awakening and my resulting discoveries is that they will provide an expanded awareness of the importance of developing a solid, centered, foundation within, that supports personal growth, expansion and vibrancy. I further hope that these discoveries will offer realistic guidance for creating more ease in everyday life.

I have created *Mainstream Gold Self-Awareness Solutions Ltd., mainstreamgold.com*—where you will find additional information and access to the following products:

The Core Perspective—A Framework for Self-Discovery

This includes the two components of the framework, (*The Core-Perspective—Game of Substance* and *The Core-Focused Renewal System*). Complimentary example exercises of energy renewal and core-creating are also available. You will also find a selection of self-care products. The self-care products are focused on enhancing our health and well-being in everyday life, as well as appreciating and respecting our Mother Earth.

I received formal education through a three-year Integrative Energy Healing Program offered by Langara College, located in Vancouver, British Columbia, Canada. I also participated in two twelve month online interactive group courses, focusing on deepening self-awareness in everyday life. The integration of this knowledge, combined with my personal discoveries, life experience, and reflection, have contributed to my truths.

RESOURCES
The Core Perspective—
A Framework for
Self-Discovery

Focuses on:

- **Twenty-nine solid core values**
- **The energy of the core**
- **Everyday life**

Using two complementary components:

- **The Core Perspective—Game of Substance**
- **The Core-Focused Renewal System**

These two components provide hands-on exercises for experiencing my personal discoveries as outlined in this book. Cultivating deeper self-awareness goes way beyond a purely intellectual exercise.

How conscious are you of your inner core?

How self-aware are you?

Discover who you truly are and create more ease through a strong sense of self.

The Core Perspective—
Game of Substance

Connecting to the flow of core consciousness with every move.

ABOUT THE CORE PERSPECTIVE

(Excerpt from the game package.)

The core is the central, innermost, essential, foundational part of all life. The energy of the core is pure, infinite, bright and vibrant and is infused with a knowing of solid core values. The spiral is a sacred symbol that reflects the pattern of growth and evolution that emanates from the core. The core is love. Be love.

The Core Perspective is a game about evolving in a balanced way through the connection to your core within...from the inside out and from the outside in. Each player begins with an original energetic template, or personal inner core, which holds an energy depth level and value of 1. As you journey along the path of the spiral, you will be wise to make choices to connect with the energy of the core in order to expand your depth level and value. As you venture along the path of the spiral you will encounter these choices often.

You will also land on insights that bring valuable levels of clarity and even breakthroughs. These insights may bring wake-up calls and the unexpected. Along the path you will also encounter blocks to your progress as you land on patterns of thought and behavior that no longer serve you. Depending on the density levels of these patterns they will slow your growth and expansion to varying degrees. These patterns may also allow for core consciousness tests and select opportunities, however, that could actually enhance your progress.

You will also be given many opportunities along the way to acquire value $ bills in order to build your material value. You will soon realize that as you build your depth perception, or energetic depth and true clarity values, your opportunities to build your material value will increase as well, and of course your substance level which is the goal of the game. Substance level as defined in the game is depth perception (energetic depth value multiplied by true clarity value) plus material value.

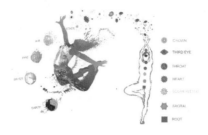

	CROWN
	THIRD EYE
	THROAT
	HEART
	SOLAR PLEXUS
	SACRAL
	ROOT

The Core-Focused
Renewal System

**Providing a "knowing" system of tuning inward
and looking outward.**

Your past and your future are reflected in the present moment. Choose to experience each moment fully engaged.

The fundamental aspect of balancing, centering and aligning, is to consciously engage with the naturally ongoing process of daily energy renewal by inviting yourself to:

- "Tap into" the core of your energy body on a daily basis.

- Dissipate/clear blocks (*dense matter*) created by patterns of thought and behavior that no longer serve you.

- Make way for increased flow and balance of your energy body.

It is natural to consciously "attune inward," so it gets easier and easier to see, feel, and know your inner truths and to incorporate them into your daily life. It is learning by doing and believing by seeing, feeling, and knowing for yourself.

THE BASIS OF THIS SYSTEM

- That the flow of life force energy and solid core values go hand in hand.

- That we come into this life with a knowing, at our core, of these values.

- That the balance and flow of energy determines our own level of health and well-being.

THE INTENT OF THIS SYSTEM

- To rediscover the relationship between life force energy and solid core values.

- To rediscover your true essence.

- To believe in yourself.

- To enjoy your uniqueness.

- To move into who and what you are becoming...to manifest your destiny.

- To trust in the unfolding.

THE FOCUS OF THIS SYSTEM

- To energetically allow the root of a current question, issue, problem, challenge, or desire to emerge.

- To support the natural shifting and realigning of your energy body that will occur as a result.

- To support the conscious awareness of this shifting, how it is being reflected in your current level of health and well-being, and how it is being manifested in your current reality.

OVER and ABOVE, to give you tools to enhance your health and well-being on many levels, this system enables you to enhance the connection/bond to the children in your life and the "child within" in a very empowering and "freeing" way.

FOUR TOOLS OF THE CORE-FOCUSED RENEWAL SYSTEM

BACK TO THE CORE WITHIN GUIDANCE CARDS—Creating space/openings/expansion *(activating responses rather than reactions)*. This is the "key ingredient" when interrelating with children. Interrelating with children involves a high level of "response-ability."

Use this package of sixty cards as your **compass**. These cards will always keep you pointed in the right direction—to your core within. A strong inner core will keep you connecting to children and the child, purity, and knowing within in a very empowering and freeing way.

BACK TO THE BASICS GUIDE TO ENERGY AWARENESS—Creating balance within *(activating conscious energy balancing)*.

Use this guide as your **map** as you consciously support your system's natural motivation for balance. It measures 8½" x 11" and includes thirty-four pages. Let the guide help you understand what you already know. All of the tools, along with your inner voice, will point you towards your energy spheres or parts of yourself that may need amplifying or attention. Balance is the key to support the free-flowing nature of energy.

BACK TO THE BASICS WORKBOOK FOR ENERGY RENEWAL—Developing depth and inner strength *(activating the connection to your driving force and your solid foundation).*

Use this workbook for **accountability**. It is a convenient way to engage with the core value exercise. It measures 5 ½" x 8 ½" and includes forty-two exercises and summaries. The core value exercise and summary may also be found on pages twenty-one and twenty-two of the guide. The exercise helps you to connect to your core within, and the summary helps you to notice and to track patterns. Use pressure/growth situations to connect with your core values and your core, in an effort to move forward in your life in a solid way.

BACK TO THE BASICS WORKBOOK FOR CORE-CREATING— Embodying the core as we create *(supporting the process of manifesting your heart's desires).*

Use this workbook for **consciousness**. It is a convenient way to engage with the core-creating exercise. It measures 5 ½" x 8 ½" and includes forty-two exercises and summaries. The core-creating exercise and summary may also be found on pages twenty-three and twenty-four of the guide. The exercises help you to generate the feelings/vibration of joy in relation to your desires and help you recognize the ways in which you are still in resistance to them. The summary helps you to notice and to track patterns. Use desires that come from your heart to manifest the life of your dreams.

Twenty-Nine Solid Core Values

Attunements

(Based on my own personal attunement.)

ENERGY SPHERES	CORE VALUES
Crown Chakra/Vortex	Appreciation
Third Eye Chakra/Brow Center	Insightfulness
Throat Chakra/Ether Center/ Ether Element	Integrity, Neutrality, Personal Truths, Respectfulness, Trustworthiness
Heart Chakra/Air Center/ Air Element	Compassion, Empathy, Faithfulness, Fidelity, Kindness, Openness

Solar Plexus Chakra/Fire Center/Fire Element	Honesty, Honor, Justice, Perseverance, Resiliency, Understanding
Sacral Chakra/Water Center/ Water Element	Allowing, Flexibility, Forgiveness, Releasing
Root Chakra/Earth Center/ Earth Element	Courage, Humility, Patience, Personal Boundaries, Supportiveness
Base Vortex	Acceptance

Twenty-Nine Solid Core Values
Definitions

(Definitions have been compiled from a variety of dictionaries. My personal preferences have been taken into consideration.)

Acceptance—a person's assent to the reality of a situation (*it is what it is*); recognizing a process or condition without trying to change it, protest, or exit.

Allowing—grant as one's right; holding space for yourself and others; to acknowledge or concede.

Appreciation—recognition of the quality, value, significance, or magnitude of people and things.

Compassion—the understanding of suffering leading to an active desire to help relieve another's suffering; gives rise to the Golden Rule: Do to others what you would have them do to you.

Courage—the ability to confront fear, pain, uncertainty or intimidation; to act rightly in the face of popular opposition or discouragement.

Empathy—to recognize emotions that are being experienced by another being; or have experienced them first hand; to be able to feel for another person.

Faithfulness—steady in allegiance or affection; loyal; constant.

Fidelity—quality of being faithful or loyal; often associated with an absence of adultery.

Flexibility—willing or disposed to yield; being able to adjust to variable circumstances.

Forgiveness—the cessation (*ending*) of judgment or hard feelings (*as a result of a perceived offense or mistake*) towards another or yourself; to be granted without expectation in order to move on.

Honesty—being truthful, fair and sincere; exhibiting straight-forward conduct.

Honor—to be true to your personal bonds; to recognize how your personal dignity and strong character can help uphold another.

Humility—modest opinion of one's overall importance in the grand scheme of things; to be grounded.

Insightfulness—to perceive beyond the obvious; to see the true nature of things, situations and people; to look inward for solutions.

Integrity—the state of being whole and undivided; being reflective of your higher self or inner voice.

Justice—to connect with moral rightness and a strong desire to be ethical and fair with yourself and others.